THE
TEEN
ANXIETY
GUIDEBOOK

THE TEEN ANXIETY

GUIDEBOOK

IMPROVE SELF-ESTEEM, DISCOVER NEW COPING SKILLS, AND RELIEVE SOCIAL ANXIETY, WORRY, AND PANIC ATTACKS

DR. THOMAS MCDONAGH AND
JON PATRICK HATCHER

BLOOM BOOKS
FOR YOUNG READERS

Published by:
Bloom Books for Young Readers
an imprint of Ulysses Press
PO Box 3440
Berkeley, CA 94703
www.ulyssespress.com

ISBN: 978-1-64604-504-4
Library of Congress Catalog Number: 2023930764

Printed in the United States by Sheridan Books Minnesota
10 9 8 7 6 5 4 3 2 1

Acquisitions editor: Claire Sielaff
Managing editor: Claire Chun
Project editor: Renee Rutledge
Proofreader: Barbara Schultz
Front cover design: Ashley Prine
Illustrations: Peter L. Brown
Layout: Winnie Liu

To my family, for all their love and support.
—Dr. Thomas McDonagh

To James and JoAnn Hatcher, Marian Lamb, and Dave Peterson for your selfless dedication to others.
—Jon Patrick Hatcher

CONTENTS

CHAPTER 1

AM I LOSING MY MIND, OR IS THIS THAT ANXIETY THING?

I am a little acorn as plain as you can see. But remember that the mighty oak was once a nut like me.

DO I HAVE ANXIETY?

I cowrote this book with Dr. McDonagh largely because of the experiences I had with anxiety as a teenager. Though I have always been a steadfast athlete and competitor, I lack grace in my day-to-day endeavors. I attribute this to an anxious mind that was always diverted to everything but what I was doing at the moment. It began when I was a child with a series of unfortunate events:

o I cracked my chin while trying to stand atop a large, plastic ball to impress my German shepherd.

- I got sick after eating granulated dishwasher detergent from under the kitchen sink. I was curious to know what it tasted like.
- I was electrocuted after touching an electric fence at a family friend's ranch during a rainstorm.
- In the fourth grade, I broke my left hand and received my first concussion during a single recess period.
- I broke my left foot doing a flip into the shallow end of a pool, and I ruptured an eardrum while scuba diving in Monterey, California.

Most of my cuts, breaks, abrasions, and contusions are directly attributed to my anxiety. Early on, I earned the nickname "Trainwreck" because of my propensity to turn so many things into worst-case scenarios. Anxiety was driving the train. When faced with any choice bigger than white or wheat, I was paralyzed by analysis. Even with sports and recreational activities, I regularly let fear and anxiety disrupt my focus and confidence, leading to personal injury and surgeries. For example, while mountain biking downhill one Saturday, I noticed a deep rut running parallel to me in the trail. I worried that my front tire would drift into the rut, causing me to flip. A reasonable fear. Except that I became fixated on the rut as I careened downhill, staring at it until my tire followed my eyes right into the small trench. I immediately tried to turn out of it, causing the wheel to buckle and the bike to somersault—with me on it. Had I kept my eyes and focus on the 80 percent of rut-less trail in front of me, I would have made it just fine. I created what I most feared by letting fear navigate.

Anxiety can make you feel different. And not in a good way. Back then, I never knew why no one else seemed to struggle with decisions or life events the way I did. And it wouldn't have mattered what diagnosis or label was put on me because it would not have changed how I felt.

Anxiety attacks in Little League and high school were my status quo, and I chalked them up to personal freak-outs. Maybe I'll outgrow them, I thought. In the absence of any deep self-realization, I always knew I was wired differently from others. And not in a cool way, like having a cloak of invisibility or being able to down an extra-large pizza in one sitting; rather, I have the powers of hypervigilance and social awkwardness.

It was bad enough that I never knew what was wrong with me; but when others openly wondered, I became self-conscious on top of feeling cracked. Fortunately, I wasn't successful at hiding my neurosis from my parents for long, since that's what parents do—pay attention and stuff. They began inquiring about my thoughts and feelings early on. When my answers surprised and scared them, they wisely found me a therapist. Therapy was cool to me as a kid because it meant going to someone's kick-ass playroom full of toys I'd never have and renting them for 50 minutes. It wasn't as cool for my parents because they didn't get to play and had to pay. If there was a form of play therapy for adults, I think a lot more people would seek help. We could play fantasy football, online poker, or Jenga. The therapist I see today has no toys. She could at least get a small sandbox with a tiny rake, or a lava lamp. But it forces me to talk, interact, and qualify my feelings without distractions, and I reap the incredible value it provides me.

> *I've got 99 problems and 93 of them are completely made-up scenarios in my head that I'm stressing about for absolutely no logical reason.*

My therapy began at 13. With some mild effort, I developed a ton of invaluable skills to counter my anxiety and even depression. Through regular application, I became a master at using cognitive behavioral therapy (CBT) and dialectical behavioral therapy (DBT) skills. Don't get lost in the acronyms, though. CBT is nothing more than a set of learned cognitive skills to solve current problems by changing unhelpful thinking and behavior (see page 32). DBT is a type of CBT psychotherapy developed in the late 1980s by psychologist Marsha M. Linehan (see page 34).

The skills I learned and developed to manage and lessen my anxiety are the same tools we teach you within this book. Additionally, they are the skills Dr. McDonagh and other therapists teach in therapy. Sitting with a stranger in talk therapy may feel awkward at first. But if you think of the therapist as a soundboard and proponent who has your best interests in mind, it'll put you more at ease. It's a definite advantage to have an impartial third party in your life, whether that person is a therapist, school counselor, or spiritual leader. Therapy is similar to strength training, in that you get out what you put in.

Everyone can benefit from talk therapy. Most of us regularly bounce ideas off of friends and seek advice from those closest to us. A therapist is a 100 percent dedicated, professional resource to provide objective help and advice. The most powerful and successful people on the planet—from executives and athletes to the president—have professional advisors guiding them.

Sadly, teenagers can let anxiety steer them through most life decisions. This can put you squarely where you don't want to be. Left untethered, anxiety will drive every choice and action you take. Rather than recognizing early on what was influencing me, I simply made thousands of questionable decisions not knowing why I constantly repeated harmful patterns that kept me stagnant or moving in reverse. You can help beat anxiety symptoms simply by knowing them, acknowledging them, and calling them out by name when they arise. "Hey, this must be my 'ole pal Anxiety creeping back in."

Anxiety is a bully you've got to constantly stand up to, or it'll be your personal shot-caller.

RECOGNIZING ANXIETY

So how do you know if you're experiencing anxiety or something more insidious with a Latin name in the Physician's Desk Reference? See "Criteria for Anxiety" on page 8.

The type of anxiety we address in this book is not the healthy, normal variety that prompts you to get important stuff done, like studying for an exam or running from clowns. The anxieties we review here go beyond the brief, beneficial kind that consist of typical worry and fear.

According to the National Institute of Mental Health (NIMH), "Severe anxiety that lasts at least six months is generally considered to be a problem that might benefit from evaluation and treatment. Each anxiety disorder has different symptoms, but all the symptoms cluster around excessive, irrational fear, and dread." Rather than motivating you to take action and get things done, anxiety at this level interferes with daily living, activities, and relationships. While some symptoms, such as worry and fear, occur in all anxiety disorders, each disorder has its own unique symptoms.

In addition to the stuff you feel in your head with an anxiety disorder, there are many physical signs of anxiety, which can include:

- Heart palpitations/pounding heart.
- Excessive sweating/ perspiration.

- Tremors or trembling/shaking or feeling weak.
- Hyperventilating or feeling like you can't catch your breath.

- Choking sensations/difficulty swallowing.
- Stomach pain, nausea, or vomiting.
- Dizziness/lightheadedness.
- Hot and cold flashes.
- Frequent urination or diarrhea.
- Muscle aches or tension.
- Headaches.
- Fatigue.
- Insomnia or problems staying asleep.
- Eating too little or too much.

Like a buffet and sneeze guard go together, anxiety and depression disorders are often interlinked. "It's very hard to find patients who are depressed who don't also have anxiety. It's equally hard to find people with anxiety that don't have some depression," says Charles Goodstein, MD, a professor of psychiatry at New York University School of Medicine with a clinical practice in Tenafly, New Jersey. So don't berate yourself if you're feeling depressed on top of everything else. It's more likely than not to occur. And though signs of depression, anxiety disorder, and even bipolar disorder have similarities, each requires different treatments right down to the medications used. This is why a professional diagnosis is so important in order to obtain the correct treatment regimen. Having anxiety doesn't have the social stigma it once did. It means you're really living.

The human body is 80 percent water, so we are basically cucumbers with anxiety.

—Unknown

TAKE CARE OF YOUR MIND, IT'S THE ONLY ONE YOU'VE GOT

We are trained as children to get good grades, get a good job, get a good spouse, get children, get ahead. In all this getting we get something else: anxiety and depression.

—Peter McWilliams, author

DR. TOM'S TAKE

The unsettling thing about having anxiety is, if you don't know it's anxiety, you start to feel like you're losing your mind. As Jon described, during these moments, it doesn't take much for things to start unraveling. You start to feel your heart rate increase, maybe some tightness in your chest, and a cool sweat breaking across your forehead, and suddenly your mind is full of questions you can't answer: What's wrong with me? Why is this happening? Is this a heart attack? Why can't I make it stop? Did I remember to lock the door? What if they stay mad at me forever?

That's the purpose of this book: to give you the answers and the tools you need during these anxious moments. You're not losing your mind; it's just an anxiety thing. This section will focus on the different types of anxiety, the anxious brain, and the benefits to having some "healthy" anxiety in our lives.

CRITERIA FOR ANXIETY

As a clinical psychologist, I classify anxiety into different categories using a book that has all the diagnostic criteria for mental health disorders. Now in its fifth edition, the book is called the *Diagnostic and Statistical Manual of Mental Health Disorders*, or DSM-5. I will cover some of the more common diagnostic criteria later in this chapter. Before I do I want to tell you a personal story in order to provide some perspective about diagnostic criteria for mental health disorders.

On my first day of graduate school, I was in a class called Adult Psychopathology. The purpose of this class was to teach students about all of the mental health disorders and the criteria that make up each diagnosis. After the usual introductions and going over the class syllabus, the professor told everyone to turn to page 462 of the DSM-4 and start reading. Well, page 462 in the DSM-4 lists the diagnostic criteria for obsessive-compulsive disorder (OCD). As I started reading, I could hear murmurs and not-so-silent whispers from the students in the class. They were saying things like "Oh, no" and "Well, that explains it," as well as some other four-letter words.

The reason these students who had just been accepted into a doctorate program were whispering self-defeating words to themselves is, many of them could identify with the symptoms of OCD. In that moment, everyone in that room thought they had OCD after looking at the criteria in the DSM-4. Having this initial reaction is exactly the reason the professor had us read it. Because despite being able to identify with the symptoms, nobody in that class met the criteria for OCD. They had some of the symptoms, not all of them, or the symptoms they did have were not intense enough to warrant a diagnosis. In fact, the professor would argue that in order to be a productive person in this world, you need to have some OCD traits. They are what make you a good student. You double-check your work, are detail-oriented, and have organization in your life. These are good things!

The point of this story is this: When you are looking at the criteria for anxiety, try to remember that you will likely identify with some of the symptoms. This is normal and to be expected. Plus, you need to have some anxiety in life to get stuff done. Feeling like you have some of the traits does not mean you have an anxiety diagnosis. (Besides, you need to see a licensed professional to receive a diagnosis.) The important point to remember is people only meet full criteria if they have the symptoms and those symptoms continue to interfere with their day-to-day life. If you feel like this is the case, then I suggest that in addition to reading this book, it could be helpful to reach out to a mental health professional. More on that in the next chapter.

The other point I would like to emphasize is that when it comes to mental health disorders, professionals treat the person, not the diagnosis. If you do meet criteria for an anxiety disorder, it does not define you. It does not say who you are. It is not a mark on you in any way.

A diagnosis is just a guide professionals need to ensure you receive the treatment that is most appropriate for you, in much the same way a medical doctor needs to know you have a broken bone so they know to treat the broken bone and not the flu. Mental health doctors need to have an idea of what is going on for you. Remember, you are no more defined by your anxiety than you would be if you had a broken bone. It's not an expression of who you are; it's only a set of symptoms.

So, with that in mind, below are some quizzes to help you decide what area of anxiety might apply most to you. It's possible to have more than one type of anxiety. Keep in mind these quizzes are meant to be helpful guides, and are not meant to be tests to diagnose an anxiety disorder. For an official diagnosis, you would need to see a licensed professional.

Let's get started!

SOCIAL ANXIETY QUIZ

Give yourself 1 point if any of the following apply to you. Do not give yourself a point if they only happen due to alcohol or drug use.

- You usually feel a sense of fear when you have to meet new people or talk to a group.
- If you have to talk in front of a group or meet new people, you usually feel that you will embarrass yourself in some way or think others will dislike you.
- You usually feel strong physical symptoms (feeling hot, sweaty, muscle tension, blushing, confusion, dry mouth, etc.) when placed in social situations.

- You usually think it's not "normal" to feel the way you do in these situations.
- You try your best to avoid new social situations.
- Your social anxiety gets in the way of your daily routine.
- The symptoms you feel have been going on for more than six months.

If you scored a 6 or higher, it's possible you have symptoms consistent with social anxiety (SA).

Random Facts About SA

- Studies suggest social anxiety is more common in women than men, but in most clinical samples, this is not the case.
- Lifetime prevalence ranges from 3 to 13 percent.
- Usually, SA has an onset in the mid-teens, sometimes due to a history of social inhibition or shyness.
- SA is more common in those who have first-degree relatives with SA.

GENERAL ANXIETY QUIZ

Give yourself 1 point if you feel any of the following apply to you. Do not give yourself a point if they only happen due to alcohol or drug use.

- You feel you worry excessively about many different topics. (The phrase "what if" goes through your mind often.)
- These intense worry thoughts happen nearly every day.
- You find it really hard to stop or control these worry thoughts.
- You feel the following (1 point for each): restless/on edge, easily fatigued, problems focusing/mind going blank, irritability, muscle tension, sleep problems.
- Your worry thoughts get in the way of your daily life.
- The symptoms you feel have been going on for at least six months.

If you scored a 7 or higher, it's possible you have symptoms consistent with generalized anxiety disorder (GAD).

Random Facts About GAD

- In adolescents, worries are often over the following:
  - » performance at school or sports, even when not being evaluated by others
  - » punctuality
  - » catastrophic events, such as earthquakes or nuclear war
  - » overly conforming
  - » being perfect
  - » being unsure of self
  - » redoing tasks
  - » needing approval or reassurance
- The percentage of people who have symptoms for one year is 3 percent; the percentage of people who have symptoms for their entire life is 5 percent.
- In people with treatment, up to 25 percent have another anxiety disorder in addition to GAD.

PANIC DISORDER QUIZ

Give yourself 1 point if any of the following happen quickly at moments of stress and peak within 10 minutes. Do not give yourself a point if they only happen because of another medical issue or are due to alcohol or drug use.

- Pounding heart rate.
- Sweating.
- Trembling/shaking.
- Shortness of breath/feeling like you are being smothered.
- Feeling of choking.
- Chest pain or discomfort.
- Nausea.
- Feeling dizzy, unsteady, lightheaded, or faint.
- Feeling detached from yourself or your surroundings ("is this real life?" feeling).

- Fear of losing control or going crazy.
- Fear of dying.
- Numbness or tingling feeling.
- Chills or hot flashes.

If you scored a 4 or more, it's possible you have symptoms that are consistent with panic disorder (PD).

First-degree relatives of someone with PD are up to eight times more likely to develop PD.

OCD QUIZ

Give yourself 1 point for each of the following criteria you can say "yes" to. Again, don't give yourself a point if it only happens during drug or alcohol use.

OBSESSIONS
- Do you have recurrent thoughts, impulses, or images that cause you anxiety or distress?
- Are these thoughts, impulses, or images more than just excessive worries about real-life problems?
- Do you try to ignore or suppress these thoughts, impulses, or images?
- Do you believe these thoughts, impulses, or images are from your own mind (and not from a belief that someone/something is making your mind think these things)?

OR

COMPULSIONS
- Do you have repetitive behaviors (like checking) or mental acts (like counting) that you feel like you have to perform in a rule-bound, rigid way?
- Do you feel less anxiety immediately after you engage in a repetitive behavior or mental act?

DO THE FOLLOWING ALSO APPLY TO YOU?

o You feel like the obsessions or compulsions are excessive or unreasonable.

o They get in the way of your normal daily routine.

If you gave yourself a point for all the criteria for either obsessions or compulsions, and gave yourself a point for both of the last two questions, then it's possible you have symptoms similar to OCD.

NOTE: The information in these quizzes is from the diagnostic criteria in the DSM.

My life is a constant panic attack occasionally interrupted by a sandwich.

THE ANXIOUS BRAIN

This will be simple brain biology, I promise. For this description, some things are oversimplified, and the brain is more complicated than what is described below. I just want you to have a general idea of what happens.

It's easier to explain if you have a model to look at. So, in one of your hands, make a fist, with your thumb in the middle of the fist. This is going to be your model of the brain.

The wrist is the brainstem, the thumb is the limbic system (where emotions come from), and the front of the fingers is the frontal lobe (personality and thinking).

The limbic system has many pieces and is involved in many things, but it is primarily involved in our emotions. One of the pieces of the limbic system is the amygdala (there are actually two of them, one on each side of your brain). The amygdala are important because they are involved in the fight-or-flight response (aka anxiety), so think of them as the scanners that are always searching for anything that could be interpreted as dangerous.

For example, if you go up a flight of stairs at home, your breathing will become a bit more rapid and your heart rate will increase slightly. Your amygdala picks up on these changes in your body and it fires. It's kind of stupid like that, because the amygdala is like an on-and-off light switch. There is no in between. It fires or it doesn't. So anything in your body that is slightly resembling anxiety, the amygdala picks up on it and it fires its signal.

This signal follows a path in your brain to your frontal lobe. Remember, on your fist, the frontal lobe is where your fingers are. Your frontal lobe (specifically the prefrontal cortex) is responsible for many things, including your personality and your ability to think at a higher level. It is the job of the frontal lobe to interpret the signaling of the amygdala. Because the amygdala works like an on-and-off light switch, it's the job of the frontal lobe to interpret if the signal is truly dangerous or not.

In the anxious brain, the amygdala fires, because that's what the amygdala does, and the frontal lobe agrees with the amygdala. It says, "Yes, this is something to be worried about," and you end up feeling anxious.

In the non-anxious brain, the amygdala fires, because it's kinda stupid like that, and then the frontal lobe says, "Chill out. It's no big deal," and you never end up feeling anxious.

So what we aim to do in this book, through education and mental exercises, is to help train your frontal lobe to tell your amygdala to chill out.

BENEFITS TO HAVING ANXIETY IN OUR LIVES

I used to teach an anxiety skills therapy group to help people conquer their anxiety. In the first class, I would ask them, "We never want to remove all anxiety from our lives. Why?" After a few jokes ("Because you want return business"), someone would eventually say something like, "Well, if I didn't have some anxiety, I probably wouldn't have realized walking along that cliff was dangerous and I would have died," or, "If I didn't have anxiety, I probably wouldn't have studied for my classes." And this is the point. We actually need anxiety in our lives because it keeps us alive and it can be motivating. A little bit of anxiety is good! Too much of it, though, is the problem.

So, when working on your anxiety, you don't want your goal to be "Remove all anxiety from my life." Not only is that unrealistic (remember, you do have those amygdala in your brain), but it's also not helpful. A dash of healthy anxiety here and there is beneficial. How else would you be motivated to do homework on the weekends or write those college essays when you'd rather be with your friends?

With this in mind, the goal we'd like you to adopt from this book is not to remove anxiety, but to bring it down to more manageable levels. We want you to learn how to regulate it. That means working with it directly, in a nonjudgmental way, and not avoiding it or thinking it's bad or weak that you feel this way. Only by working with it directly can you bring it down to more manageable levels.

We'll talk about how to do this in the rest of the book.

WAYS TO ALLEVIATE ANXIETY

1. Accept that you are anxious in order to lessen it.

2. Rearrange the furniture in your room. A new perspective and outlook could be a welcome change.

3. Write it out. Writing is cathartic, and keeping a diary or journal of your thoughts, feelings, and emotions is one of the most effective ways to manage mood disorders.

4. Challenge your anxious thoughts and beliefs. What is the evidence? What is the worst case? What is likely? Remember this important chain: Thoughts precede feelings, which precede behaviors. Negative thoughts lead to negative emotions, which lead to negative behaviors.

5. Practice desensitization. You can counter your greatest fears and worries and desensitize yourself to them. If you fear driving on the freeway, then get on that freeway.

6. Confront the sources of your anxiety. Change what you can. Accept what you cannot.

7. Install some anxiety-related apps on your smartphone, and carry anxiety relief with you. Search for "anxiety relief"in your app store.

8. Get a touchstone. A touchstone is simply something small and smooth. You hold it in your hand and rub it gently with your thumb when you're stressed or anxious.

CHAPTER 2

VS

MEDICATION VS. THERAPY

Anxiety can try to bury you, but you're a seed.

—Unknown

IF YOU'RE ANXIOUS AND YOU KNOW IT, SHAKE YOUR MEDS

There is a little-known dichotomy about anxiety that makes seeking treatment difficult: When you're feeling anxious, it's often hard to do what's best for your welfare—this includes seeking help. My anxiety doesn't want me to pay bills until I'm getting hate mail from creditors, fold laundry until I have no room on my bed to sleep, get groceries until I'm down to ramen and a jar of crusted mayo, or wash my car until strangers spell profanities on the windows. And, while on anxiety medication, anxiety doesn't like me taking my pills regularly or at all. Anxiety is a narcissist that wants you to focus on … anxiety.

Anxiety will cloud your mind and fill your consciousness with a perverse volume of thoughts, noise, feelings, and stressors that have no validity. Meanwhile, the tasks with deadlines and consequences that need to get done get buried in the cerebral ruckus. Next thing you know, you're not turning in homework on time, missing chores, and arriving late to work or practice, and everyone's wondering why you can't get your act or matching socks together. But if they saw the thought carnival in your mind, they'd surely understand. Here are some options Dr. McDonagh and I recommend to help.

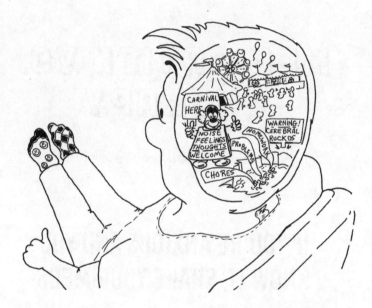

REDUCING YOUR ANXIETY THROUGH THERAPY

Most cases of anxiety disorder can be treated successfully by a mental health professional like a psychologist or therapist. Focus on the skills without worrying about their origins, categories, or acronyms. Remember, your thoughts contribute to the symptoms of your anxiety disorders. Work to change your thoughts and you can change the frequency and intensity of your anxiety. If it seems a simple idea, it is. But it takes work. Anything worthwhile does.

Countering

I can't stress enough the importance of "countering," or doing the opposite of what anxiety is pushing you to do. Countering is the single best tactic to rob anxiety of its vain tendencies. Just as a sibling or bully tries to push your buttons to solicit a reaction, so it goes with anxiety. A little reverse psychology goes a long way. If you don't counter the anxiety, you will likely experience recurring panic attacks and avoidance behavior that may create problems at work, with family, and at school. Anxiety lurks everywhere—do not mistake composure for ease.

Don't get discouraged. Just because I've chosen to spend much of my life in therapy doesn't mean you need to. My therapist is now far more of a life coach for me than anything else. She's insanely adept at assisting me with my interpersonal relationships, providing career advice, offering relaxation techniques, and helping me make sound decisions about big things like where I should move next, or reasons not to buy a pony.

The duration of therapy needed is unique for everyone. Many people experience improvement within only a few sessions, where others reap benefits through months or even years of seeing a professional. There's no commitment and your therapist works for you, with the goal of helping you achieve measurable improvement. If you don't like or work well with one psychologist, choose another. It's that simple. They won't take it personally. And if they do, they should see a therapist. I've only had one therapist I didn't like. She was always in a bad mood. One day, I walked out on our appointment and suggested that she instead pursue a role with the DMV. Not every therapist should be one.

A MEDICATED WORLD

According to *Psychology Today*, the average person seeking help today leans toward psychiatric drugs rather than psychotherapy. Antidepressants and antianxiety medications are among the leading prescription drugs in the world. These findings are echoed by Kathryn McHugh and colleagues, who found that the vast majority of people seeking treatment for depression and anxiety disorders prefer pharmcological to psychological interventions by a ratio of 3 to 1.

Psychologically, we are a medicated world. Why do you see so many lengthy, pricey commercials for anxiety drugs? Because so many people have it, and there's a huge market of potential users who equate to massive profit for drug manufacturers.

Ultimately, I agree with the expert findings that there's a place for both medication and psychotherapy in treating anxiety, and depending on the person and symptoms, for receiving them in tandem. Today, I successfully manage my anxiety using CBT-based skills usage I've learned through therapy. Meds can get you over a harmful anxiety-provoking event, such as the loss of a loved one, and they tend to work a little faster than CBT by a matter of weeks. But it's also important to learn the cognitive (aka mental) coping skills to manage anxiety long term. It is my belief that if you've been prescribed meds, it should always be combined with therapy.

Research suggests that medications often work, but only as long as you keep taking them, whereas skills-based therapy such as CBT may reduce risk for anxiety symptoms returning long after treatment is over.

Every case of anxiety is unique and one size never fits all. Unfortunately, many anxiety sufferers use prescription medication when therapy, exercise, or self-help strategies such as those taught here would work just as well, if not better, because they are actual skills with no side effects. Therapy and skills usage include development of the necessary tools to beat anxiety. No medication will cure anxiety; it treats the symptoms. Only therapy, and skills development and usage, can permanently eradicate or best manage anxiety. Though medication can greatly assist, there remains a risk that it can cause an increase, rather than a decrease, in depression and anxiety. I prefer to see medication used only after diet and lifestyle interventions when possible.

Just come away from this knowing that you have options. You never need to white-knuckle this alone. Your anxiety can make it hard to reach out, which is exactly why you need to! It gets so much better—I promise.

> *People want a quick fix, but that's not how it works. It's a whole way of looking at life, a whole way of living, taking care of yourself.*
>
> —Babette Galang, MPH, LMT, director of
> Traditional Healing & Kupuna Program at Papa Ola Lōkahi

An Important Note on the Antianxiety Supplement Kava

You may have seen or heard of kava as a natural supplement in alleviating anxiety. Kava is used frequently to treat anxiety, depression, insomnia, stress, and menopausal symptoms. But in a consumer advisory, the FDA urged people using kava who developed symptoms of liver disease to consult a physician. Subsequently, many studies have examined the safety and potential toxicity of kava.

Despite FDA warnings, kava remains an extremely popular supplement in the United States. Research has identified toxic compounds found in the stem and leaves that are not found in the kava root. The World Health Organization (WHO) has joined with the Natural Standard Research

Collaboration (NSRC) to issue an updated report on the hepatotoxicity of kava.

Because supplements are not monitored by the FDA, it's difficult to know the source and efficacy of the kava you find in stores. Do some research before purchasing. I used to take kava daily prior to learning of the potential adverse effects. I obtained no discernible improvement in my anxiety symptoms while I was on it, and I was happy to save on the $30 per bottle purchase price. That's more than my monthly gym membership, a far better use of my cash and organs.

A DAILY PROCESS

Even today, managing my anxiety is a daily—often hourly—process. If I don't have my go-to skills ready for instant execution, it can result in a troubling spike in anxiety. Take, for example, my afternoon break while writing this chapter. I took some much-needed personal time to relax and complete a couple of errands on a beautiful Sunday. What started off a blissful respite went south in just hours.

It began with a $43 parking ticket while I was grabbing lunch. Frustrating for sure, especially since I was only a few minutes late sprinting back to an expired parking meter. But things got far more expensive. My next task was to pick up my dry cleaning. Instead of being greeted by the owner I've known for years, I walked in to an older gentleman filling in while the owner was on an overseas vacation. The substitute employee had no idea what he was doing. He slowly punched some numbers into the outdated point of sale system to charge me the $57.85 I owed, printed the receipt for me to sign, and handed it to me. Except he added a "5" to the total. My receipt read "$557.85—Approved" just above the line for my signature. That was $500 extra taken straight out of my checking account. Not being familiar with the device, he had no idea how to credit the overcharge back to my card.

The power of the pause: In every instance, we have a few moments to choose our reaction to any event. This is often the difference between laughing and going to prison.

It's a short window that feels like fractions of a second. It's imperative that you insert a fat pause after anything that provokes your anxiety or anger. This tiny period should be used to reset your perspective on a difficult activating event. For example, when I first saw the $557, my gut reaction was that he was purposely stealing $500 from me. The next sensation I felt was rage, followed by the desire to perform some act of revenge. So, I paused. This gave me the instant I needed to see how best to mitigate things. Then I left everything inside and just walked out the door. Walk away from an emotional ignition source whenever possible.

You don't understand—I'm a natural worst-case scenario expert.

As I walked out, I could feel my anxiety and anger crest and then fall. But I was now safely outside where I wouldn't offend or assail anyone. I had smartly created a "zone of diffusion" where I could do no harm, beyond kicking my own car.

The invaluable pause allowed me to quickly identify what I was feeling and calm my anger and anxiety before a harmful escalation. Rather than get angry at the hapless fill-in cashier, I practiced some empathy and forgiveness, and called my bank to help resolve the accident. Removing yourself from severe anxiety-provoking stimuli is the most suitable first step. You don't need to figure anything out. You don't even need to think or use anything but your legs. Just begin walking in the other direction. I did what I could in the moment and let the rest go until the next day, while practicing that annoying but effective Serenity Prayer ("God grant me the serenity to accept the things I cannot change; courage to change the things I can; and wisdom to know the difference"). Within minutes, I was laughing about the whole scenario.

> *Before you criticize someone, you should walk a mile in their shoes. That way, when you criticize them, you are a mile away from them and have their shoes.*
>
> —Jack Handey, humorist

DR. TOM'S TAKE

PRESCRIPTION FOR EXCELLENCE

After years of treating anxiety in a clinical setting, I firmly believe medications and talk therapy are the two best treatment options. This section will discuss each option, as well as their benefits and some possible drawbacks.

As is the case with any type of treatment, the doctor or provider that works with you directly (if you see someone) is the best resource. If there is contradictory information between what you read here and what they say, you should talk about it with your doctor directly. They know you and your medical history, so they will always be the best resource for information.

If you are considering taking medications, I would strongly recommend you see a professional that specializes in treating "pediatrics with psychiatric disorders." Teenagers are different from adults in many ways, and people with a specialty in mental health are more familiar with the drugs and dosages.

WHEN TO SEE A PROFESSIONAL

There are two situations when you should start to see a professional. If either of these applies to you, then I strongly recommend that you seek professional help.

The first situation is fairly straightforward. If you are in danger of hurting yourself or others, or if you are having passive thoughts about hurting yourself or others (even if you don't have a plan or any real intent to follow through with these thoughts), then you should see someone. Depending on the intensity of these thoughts, calling 911 or 988 and asking for help could be your best option. More on this is covered in the chapter that covers self-harm and suicide.

The second situation where you should consider seeing a professional is if your symptoms are starting to interfere with your daily life. Examples of symptoms interfering with your daily life could include suddenly not getting along with friends or family, difficulty with sleep, problems eating, doing poorly at school, or starting to use alcohol or drugs to cope or feel better.

MEDICATIONS

Three different types of medications are most commonly prescribed for anxiety:

1. Benzodiazepines (BZs)
2. Selective serotonin reuptake inhibitors (SSRIs)/Serotonin-norepinephrine reuptake inhibitors (SNRIs)
3. Beta blockers

Again, this is meant to be a source of information and does not include all the facts necessary to make an informed decision about medications. That is a conversation you need to have with the person prescribing you medication.

Just so you know, there are other types of medications that treat anxiety, but they are less commonly prescribed. They include tricyclic antidepressants (TCAs), monoamine oxidase inhibitors (MAOIs), other antidepressants, mild tranquilizers, and anticonvulsants. We will not cover these medications in this chapter.

BENZODIAZEPINES

Benzodiazepines are generally prescribed for people with a diagnosed anxiety disorder, such as generalized anxiety disorder, panic disorder, obsessive compulsive disorder, or post-traumatic stress disorder. Some commonly prescribed BZs are Xanax, Klonopin, and Valium.

A nice advantage to BZs is they tend to work quickly after you take them, so people appreciate the quick relief. Also, the time frame in which you feel the effect of BZs is limited to less than a day (depending on the medication, dosage, body weight, body chemistry, etc.). So, you can either take them only when it's needed or take a prescribed amount each day.

A downside to using BZs is that if taken on a regular basis or prescribed a high dosage, your body can become dependent upon the drug. This means that if you stop taking the drug cold turkey or too quickly, you could experience withdrawal symptoms. Also, sometimes people experience "rebound anxiety" when they stop taking a BZ too quickly. Rebound anxiety is the temporary return of anxiety symptoms, where the symptoms are typically more intense than they were when you first started taking the BZ.

In rare cases, it's possible to overdose on a BZ. This is why you should only take BZ as prescribed, and not in a higher amount than your doctor intended.

SSRIS/SNRIS

SSRIs and SNRIs are both antidepressants, but don't let that confuse you. Both types of medications are helpful at treating anxiety as well. SSRIs work on a brain chemical (neurotransmitter) called serotonin. SNRIs work on both serotonin and norepinephrine, another type of neurotransmitter. Both SSRIs and SNRIs are prescribed for different types of anxiety disorders.

Common SSRIs are Prozac, Zoloft, Paxil, Lexapro, and Celexa. Common SNRIs are Effexor and Cymbalta.

These are the types of medications that you have to take every day, and often for at least two weeks (sometimes up to six weeks or more) to build up in your system. So, the immediate relief that you would have with a BZ does not happen with an SSRI or SNRI. But the advantage is that once they start taking them on a regular basis, most people tend to feel less anxiety overall. However, unlike BZs, your body does not become dependent upon them and there are no withdrawal effects (unless you stop taking them abruptly).

Sometimes people say they feel side effects that can include nausea, insomnia, headaches, feeling more irritable, as well as a possible increase in anxiety during the first two weeks of taking SSRIs/SNRIs.

BETA BLOCKERS

Beta blockers are quite effective for some types of anxiety, but they are also prescribed for people with high blood pressure. This is because beta blockers are prescribed to control the physical symptoms of high blood pressure—a rapid heart rate, shaking, trembling, and blushing—the same symptoms that can happen during stage fright, meeting new people, or social anxiety. Beta blockers work because they prevent your heart from beating too fast so your body feels calm in these situations.

Common beta blockers include Inderal, Tenormin, and Lopressor.

People generally like these medications because they are fast acting (like BZs), and by keeping your heart rate down, they prevent your body from going into fight-or-flight mode. They also are not habit-forming, so there are no withdrawal symptoms.

However, some anxiety symptoms are severe, and beta blockers do not always work. Also, medical complications can arise if you have problems with your heart or lungs, or have asthma, diabetes, or depression. This is another reason why it's important to talk to your doctor before you take any type of medication.

CHOOSING YOUR THERAPIST

There are many different types of talk therapies available, and many different types of therapists to choose from. So which therapy and therapist is right for you?

When it comes to treating all mental health issues, especially anxiety, you want to make sure you choose a therapist that uses an approach that is evidence based or empirically validated. This means that they say and do things to treat your symptoms that have been proven by research to be effective.

When choosing a therapist, there are many different types of professionals with different therapy degrees. They include psychiatrists, psychologists, and masters level therapists. When choosing a therapist, make sure the person is licensed. If they are licensed, this means they went to a school that was accredited, received training that was accredited, and have passed both a national and state licensing examination to prove they know what they are talking about.

In addition to the accreditation, you want to make sure you see someone that you like! The quality of the relationship is imperative. If you don't like the therapist, then the treatment isn't going to be as effective.

So, if you are going to see a therapist, the type of degree is less important than making sure they are licensed, practice using techniques that are supported by research, and are someone you can trust and get along with.

EVIDENCE-BASED THERAPIES

COGNITIVE BEHAVIORAL THERAPY (CBT)

This is the most researched and effective therapy for treating anxiety issues. CBT works to change thoughts and behaviors that cause mental health symptoms. To achieve this goal, a CBT therapist typically breaks anxiety down into three different buckets: physical symptoms, thoughts, and behaviors.

Physical symptoms of anxiety can include rapid breathing and heart rate, dizziness, hot/cold flashes, blushing, or tunnel vision, among other symptoms. The treatment for these symptoms usually includes what is called relaxation skills. This can include breathing exercises, progressive muscle relaxation, grounding techniques, or other skills that focus on calming your body and switching it out of flight-or-flight mode.

CBT defines three layers to our thoughts.

- First layer. Thoughts and feelings you are having in the moment that you are aware of. For example: When I am driving and get cut off on the highway, the feeling and thought I am aware of is: I am upset and think the driver that cut me off is an *expletive*.

- Second layer. These are called automatic thoughts because they happen automatically, almost like a reflex. These are the thoughts that create the first layer thoughts. Think of the second layer as the expectations/rules we live by. They are usually about ourselves, other people, and our future. When these rules don't match up with the reality that happens to us, it creates the feelings and thoughts in the first layer. The second-layer thoughts can be easily identified because they typically include words like "must," "should," "always," "never," "ought to." For example: Other people should not cut me off on the highway.

- Third layer. These are the "unconscious" thoughts. They are our core values. Our core values are developed early in life when we are young and our frontal lobes (that do high-level thinking) can only see us, other people, and our world in black-and-white terms. As a result, all people develop core values based on black-and-white ideas. These core values create rules/expectations, which then influence how we feel and think in the moment. For example: I am loveable/I am not loveable. I have worth/I don't have worth. People are good/people are bad.

To put it all together using the driving example: Someone cuts me off on the highway. I feel upset (first layer). Why? Because people shouldn't cut me off on the highway (second layer). Why? Because it means that they don't care about me, and I need everyone to care about me to have worth (third layer).

Anxiety Thoughts

When it comes to anxiety specifically, the automatic thoughts (second layer) associated with anxiety are always going to be about danger, or worst-case-scenario situations. Different techniques are used to challenge these thoughts. They can include reframing, challenging statements, working with cognitive distortions, or many other skills.

Behaviors associated with anxiety are always going to be about avoidance. Sometimes, the avoidance is intentional; other times it's unintentional. The thing to remember is the more you avoid, the more you reinforce the anxiety. So the goal is to change the behavior, stop avoiding, and expose yourself gradually to the anxiety-provoking situation. Now, this does not mean you should jump into the deep end of the pool. There is a very procedural and systematic way to approach these situations and desensitize you to the anxiety trigger. Using the relaxation skills you learn, there are different types of "exposure therapies." For example, developing a situational hierarchy is useful for phobias, using interoceptive exposure is helpful for panic disorder, and role playing is great for communication issues.

Breathe. You're going to be okay. Breathe and remember that you've been in this place before. You've been this uncomfortable and anxious and scared, and you've survived. Breathe and know that you can survive this too. These feelings can't break you. They're painful and debilitating, but you can sit with them and eventually they will pass. Maybe not immediately, but sometime soon. They are going to fade, and when they do, you'll look back at this moment and laugh for having doubted your resilience. I know it feels unbearable right now, but keep breathing again and again. This will pass. I promise It Will Pass.

—Daniell Koepke, founder of the online space
Internal Acceptance Movement (I. A.M.)

DIALECTICAL BEHAVIOR THERAPY (DBT)

Dialectical behavior therapy (developed by Marsha M. Linehan) is an empirically validated treatment that is intensive, but also measurably effective. In a true DBT program, an individual agrees to be in treatment for a certain period of time (usually a year). This yearlong commitment includes group therapy and individual therapy weekly. Over the course of the year, the individual learns skills that focus on four topics: mindfulness, interpersonal effectiveness, distress tolerance, and emotional regulation. For each topic, there are several skills that build on each other. Each topic takes about three months to go through. It is not unusual for participants to complete several rounds (a few years!) of DBT.

There will be many skills in this book that reference evidence-based techniques. Remember as you read along that these skills are supported by research and are found to be helpful at reducing anxiety symptoms.

WAYS TO ALLEVIATE ANXIETY

9. Time how long you can hold your breath, and work to beat your previous time each attempt.

10. Learn how to cook or bake something that is somewhat challenging.

11. Listen to a podcast or TED talk.

12. Look up something new about art. Even better, visit your local museum.

13. Roll tennis balls under your bare feet. It feels great!

14. Chew gum. Believe it or not, chewing gum reduces cortisol levels and eases stress. Make it sugarless.

15. Use meditation rather than medication, where applicable (prescription or otherwise). Scientists are discovering that meditation actually increases the amount of gray matter in the brain, essentially rewiring the body to stress less.

16. Hug it out. Hugs are free therapy. They also reduce blood pressure and stress.

CHAPTER 3

TEENS AND TECH

Technology is often what stands between teens and humanity.

MY BEST FRIENDS ARE EMOJIS

Dr. McDonagh and I grew up in an era not known for leaps in technological advances. The lack of fun lithium ion-powered iThings forced my peers and me to engage in more traditional pastimes like fishing, playing with LEGO sets, going outside, sniffing markers, and even reading. There were cool video games available outside the mall arcades, but only the spoiled kids had them, while I fumbled with my low-tech Lite-Brite and Etch A Sketch.

Even if my parents wanted to fill our home with the latest electronic gadgetry, it wouldn't happen until everything else we could play with became unsalvageable. My dad could repair anything, and not once was a repairman called to the house. The drawback was that I never got anything new. Even today my dad rarely discards anything.

If someone in the family wanted something gone, it had to be covertly disassembled, stealthily removed from the house under the cover of night, and buried under the existing garbage in a trash bin outside. It was best to do this at 3:30 a.m. on the morning of trash pickup at the risk he'd notice something of potential value was tossed. Otherwise, he'd remove the object from the trash and it would be repaired, cleaned, and placed in its original location. "As good as new!" he would proclaim as we sighed in disappointed unison, giving up the hope of ever going to a store.

I'd like to think that if social media were as prevalent in my teen years as it is today, my dad would've limited us to walkie-talkies so we'd never regret an online post or selfie. Nor would we succumb to online bullying. We happily kept our screwups face to face and with limited audiences. I'm incredibly thankful I had no access to social media as a kid. I made enough bad decisions without access to offend the masses. Knowing how reliant teens are on social media and apps today, I am sure I would have experienced far more anxiety and drama as a teen. Fortunately, I could only wreak limited havoc by crank calling people from a wall-mounted telephone.

THE PROS AND CONS OF TEEN SOCIAL MEDIA USE

I'm a fan of social and business media networking—to a degree. I find the more time I spend on any social media site, the more aggravated I become with things posted by others. But I also learn a lot from particular pages and organizations that I follow.

Studies point to some quality benefits provided by social networking, such as:

- Augments and manages your social life.
- Provides a simpler way for socially anxious teens to communicate.
- Helps teens with life challenges or disabilities to connect with others for support.
- Provides access to sources of employment, outdoor activities, or social opportunities.
- Creates a means of reacquainting with old or distant friends, or family who live far away.

There are also downsides to social media for teens, specifically generating additional anxiety and depression. In many ways technology has dehumanized relationships. This is not meant to be a lecture, rather data points for you to consider. Studies and surveys reveal that social networking exposes you to certain disadvantages and risks, including some of the following:

- Lots of drama.
- Cyberbullying and harassment by peers.
- Online predators.
- Less personal interaction with family and others.
- Identity theft and exposure to external intrusions, hacking, and viruses.
- Isolation and replacement of valuable face-to-face time.
- Considerable time and productivity often wasted.
- Proliferation of false or misleading information.
- Regrettable posts or photos that cannot be redacted.
- Potential negative impact on college acceptance or employment prospects.
- Less time outdoors being active while enabling laziness.
- Can lead to stress and offline relationship problems.
- Correlated with a need for instant gratification, ADHD, addictive disorders, and self-centered personalities.
- Unexpected proliferation of personal images.
- Receiving hack advice and self-diagnosis for issues requiring actual professional help.
- Creates an impetus to try to remain relevant and popular.

WHY PEOPLE BULLY

Those who bully in any form dislike themselves and project their self-loathing onto others. Deep down, they are unhappy cowards. They wouldn't bully someone bigger or badder than they are at the risk of an imminent beatdown. So they prey on those they perceive to be weaker.

How we treat other people always comes back to us. If someone bullies or treats you poorly, there is something wrong with them, not you. Normal people don't get pleasure from destroying others. Only hurt people will hurt people. The love that comes back to us in life is the love that we express. Take the high road and try not to remind them what a sad sack they are.

There is overwhelming evidence that the higher the level of self-esteem, the more likely one will be to treat others with respect, kindness, and generosity.
—Nathaniel Branden, author of *The Six Pillars of Self-Esteem*

Most people bully to feel more important or popular. They may bully out of jealousy toward you. Or, it may be to escape their own problems, such as being bullied themselves. Targeting and picking on someone else makes them feel big and powerful. Inside, they feel neither. And they typically target those who are different or otherwise don't fit in. This is not an invitation to try to blend in! Always be yourself, and be proud of this version of you.

Boys frequently bully using physical threats and actions, while girls are more likely to engage in verbal or relationship bullying, but the results are similar. Sticks and stones may break bones, but words will only cause permanent psychological damage.

Here are seven tactics to assuage a bullying situation:

1. Avoid contact if possible.
2. Stand up for yourself, but—more importantly—protect yourself.
3. Have a friend and be a friend—there is strength in numbers. Be more than a bystander.
4. Don't bully back.
5. Don't show emotion.
6. Tell an adult in authority.

7. Find the humor. Everyone knows how arcane and ridiculous bullying and bullies are.

Remember that bullies are hurt, unhappy people that want you to be equally miserable. Don't give them that satisfaction by letting them dictate your own agenda. Chances are you're dealing with someone who didn't get enough hugs from their mommy.

Bullying is often a learned behavior, and kids can be both victim and bully simultaneously. It's not your job to fix them, but there's often an opportunity to find the common ground. This doesn't mean redirecting your bully to another victim and then jointly harassing them. I'll give you an example.

A few years ago at my public gym, there was a group of loud, boisterous guys who lifted weights daily. This particular group consisted of six former members of a notorious street gang in my area. This was evident from their tattoos and what I was told by others who knew them. More than one of them had done stints in prison.

My girlfriend at the time would work out with me on weekends, and on a few occasions I overheard the guys make sexual comments about her. This infuriated me. I let them know I heard them by my glances, which they shot back with impunity. They were unfriendly but did not make threats. Everything was implied. I was out of my element with this motley crew.

Beyond that, I knew better than to engage or mutter a word. Instead, I vowed to befriend them over time under the premise "If you can't beat 'em, join 'em." Or get beat up and then join them.

You can't always find commonalities with your tormentor. And I don't recommend this approach without some skills in street diplomacy. But a tactic that a close girlfriend of mine, Shelbie, used in high school was obtaining sympathy from her female bully. Shelbie was being verbally and physically harassed after school each week by a much larger, angry girl in the same grade. Shelbie decided to have a neutral third party tell her aggressor that her dad was gravely ill and fighting to survive, and to please have compassion for her and stop the bullying. It worked.

Shelbie risked creating some common ground in the form of potential empathy. The bully had a conscience and decided that Shelbie probably had more hardship than herself, so she moved on and bullied someone else. (A few someone elses, sadly.) That's what bullies do—they move on to indiscriminately harass others on a whim. Whatever bullying you might be experiencing is temporary. At some point, they will move on, get bullied themselves, or get into serious trouble.

We get that you want to save face and not look weak or scared, or possibly worsen the bullying by telling someone. But you can't take on the world, nor should you. No matter how badass someone thinks they are, there is always someone ready to take them on. And it shouldn't be you. Your job is to stay safe and protect your physical and emotional well-being. And seeking help from the authorities is a sound part of that plan. For additional helpful information go to www.StopBullying.gov.

Growing up in school no one ever called me anything close to an innovator. They called me "different," they called me "weird," they called me a couple other things I can't say here. Thankfully my mother taught me that being different was a good thing … that being different meant you could actually make a difference.

—Justin Timberlake, singer and actor

FEEL LIKE SEXTING? TWO WORDS: "REVENGE PORN"

Recent studies have found that sexting is considered "normal" when it comes to adolescent sexual behavior. This is unfortunate, as sexting is typically a bad idea between most anyone beyond consenting, married adults. Even then there's a risk of content or photos ending up in the wrong place.

We live in an age where one tiny lapse in judgment can last forever in the cloud. The repercussions are irreversible and far beyond anyone's control. And the future consequences run the gamut from negatively impacting college admissions, to losing out on a job due to what a prospective employer finds when they Google you, to the potential impact to your lifelong personal reputation. It's best to hold a zero-tolerance stance on sexting, no matter how much someone begs you to do it. The risk does not justify any momentary reward.

In the majority of cases, a risqué photo ends up where it was meant to. But it only takes one time to be wrong. Social networks have created an environment where there is a perceived duty to expose yourself. Don't.

According to surveys, some of the primary reasons teenagers send sexually explicit photos include:

- Pressure from a peer.
- Romantic interest or as a romantic gesture.
- Cyberbullying.
- Low self-esteem.

- Seeking independence or acting in defiance.
- As a sexual favor in exchange for something else.

And don't think using "safer" and anonymous chat apps that erase your bad decision after hitting "send" will protect you. It only takes a second for a recipient to grab a screenshot. Keep in mind that sending sexts of anyone under 18 years of age is illegal—even if it's a pic of you.

Studies have shown that girls are slightly more likely to send explicit photos than boys. This is probably because boys are far more persistent at conning girls into sending them. But before you do, ask yourself one thing: Is this a photo I won't mind my parents, friends, classmates, and total strangers seeing? Because there's a chance they will.

No matter what they say, guys love to share this stuff with other guys to gain popularity or notch up their cred. Be more intriguing and attractive by being mysterious. If you want to keep someone's interest, don't give them all the goods, and save your integrity.

REVENGE PORN

Re•venge porn, noun. A form of sexual abuse that involves the distribution of nude/sexually explicit photos and/or videos of an individual without their consent. Revenge porn, sometimes called cyber-rape or non-consensual pornography, is usually posted by a scorned ex-lover or friend, in order to seek revenge after a relationship has gone sour.

Source: www.EndRevengePorn.org

The only way revenge porn doesn't affect you is if you never text a single nude selfie. Otherwise it could play out as it does for so many other victims (especially females). You might think it won't happen to you. You're in a monogamous relationship and your boyfriend convinces you to send some sexy, revealing pics. You're not comfortable with it, but you love and trust him. You text "BRB" and begin taking your best versions of some risqué pics to pique his sexual interest. Your pics are well received—he loves them. Yaaaay! But he wants more. And more. And more. That's how us guys work; we're greedy and insatiable. And we'll connive to get what we want. So if you never send the first one, you'll never be pestered endlessly to send more … and more.

One photo. 515 shares. 988 comments. Online forever.

Fast forward a few months, and your once-perfect relationship is on the rocks. He wasn't everything you thought he was in the beginning, so you try to talk to him about your feelings. But it turns into a big argument, and things quickly end badly with him turning cold and mean because that's just how some people break up. Later, it hits you: "OMG! What about all those naked selfies of me on his phone?!" Exactly. What about those? Sure, he promised not to show anyone; but within a few weeks, you're getting side eyes from classmates at school. Then your best friend sends a text to you stating that your once-private pics are circulating among guys at school. A lot of guys.

At the time of this writing, 48 states and the District of Columbia have revenge porn laws in place, with many states classifying aggravating factors or a second offense as a felony. In a growing number of states the first offense is a felony. As it should be. But no law can take back what's already out there or undo what you feel. In the end, it's not just revenge, and it's not just porn. It's one of the deepest betrayals of trust by a partner or ex. And the only protection is not gifting that first pic. You'll never regret what you don't send.

The key takeaway is that there are three potential outcomes from your sexting:

1. You get away with it with no consequences. You get lucky.
2. It gets out and goes viral. You're buried in regret.
3. You proliferate child pornography. You're buried in regret.

CYBERBULLYING TIPS

Even as I (Jon) pen this section, I've been dealing with an online bully. Some adults never outgrow being a tyrant. This particular troll has been stalking me via social media to harass and insult me simply because he didn't agree with the premise of an article I published. The best part is that he completely misunderstood the article's theme, and that it actually bolstered his perspective. But haters don't need to be right, they just need to hate on something or someone to feed their own self-loathing.

Whenever I blocked him, he would create a new profile under a fake name and renew his sad campaign. As much as I wanted to call him out on his stupidity, I ignored him entirely, thereby robbing any satisfaction he might obtain. And that's all he wanted—to be validated. Not getting what he wanted, he disappeared. I'm sure he's off haranguing someone else in his quest for attention.

As in real life, don't respond to the comments of a cyberbully. Providing a response gives the person or people more material to work with. Plus there's a good chance if you respond it's going to be with something that is emotionally driven and not something you'd actually do. Stating things like "I'll kill you" or "I'll beat your ass" on social media, even if you don't mean it, can land you in serious trouble. It's actually a prosecutable crime. It's best to not respond at all.

Document and save as much evidence as you can. Take screenshots or use any other means you can think of to collect and save the material. Try to find a way to get a date and time stamps of the evidence as well. This way, you have something specific you can give to authorities to make it stop. Which brings us back to …

Tell someone. Again, you are not being a rat. Besides telling an adult you trust, you can also contact the social media site directly. Cyberbullying is taken extremely seriously, and most platforms have strong policies preventing abusive material being on their sites or directed at their users. If you contact the company, there's a solid chance they'll remove it right away.

Remember, be careful what information or pictures you send to friends or post on social media. You might think you can trust someone now, but there's always a chance that something could happen down the line, and that person could use the picture to embarrass you. If you don't put anything out there, there won't be anything for people to use against you. As a measure, try not to send anything over the internet that you wouldn't want your parents to see.

SOCIAL MEDIA: COMPARING OUR LIVES TO THE ONLINE LIVES OF OTHERS

Hopefully you know this, but it's worth repeating: People's real lives are nowhere near as grand as their social media "lives." It's a total myth. Their real lives are much less flattering. "Here I am at home cleaning my cat's litter box and doing my assigned chores." "Now it's Saturday night and I'm home watching reels and trimming my cuticles." Not as glamorous, right?

There's no shortage of stories of people faking or distorting settings, events, and truths to create and sustain a false persona. People can go beyond deep fakes and create synthetic media. Essentially, you can use anyone's body and face to make them say anything, anywhere, at any time. And not always for entertainment or to instill envy.

Consider influencer Natalia Taylor who has millions of online followers. In 2020, she posted a series of Instagram photos that seemed to show her relishing a lavish vacation at a resort in Bali, Indonesia. She later revealed, however, that the photos were taken at her local Ikea as part of a ploy she staged to show people that life online isn't always what it seems. Well played.

In addition to these stories, there are studies that show actually looking at other people's lives on social media makes us feel worse. One such study from 2019 used the "Instagram vs. Reality" trend to test the impact of photos on body image in young women. The study divided the women participants into two groups. One group looked at the idealized Instagram images, and the other group looked at less glamorized "reality" images. The results of the study were predictable. The women that looked at the idealized images had an increase in body dissatisfaction (they felt worse about their bodies). Whereas the women that looked at the reality images had less body dissatisfaction (they felt better about their bodies).

What should you take away from this study? Know that looking at idealized social media pictures will make you feel worse about yourself, so you should treat these images with caution. If you find yourself scrolling through glamorized images, remind yourself they are a produced product that are far from reality.

Social media is the new permanent record.

It's the old compare-and-despair dilemma. We are curious, so we look, and then we feel bad. If you feel like it's an unstoppable cycle, then the behavior parallels obsessiveness. In OCD, people feel an increase in anxiety or distress, so they engage in a compulsive behavior, which provides relief in the short term. This relief or decrease in anxiety is what reinforces the compulsive behavior in the brain. The brain thinks, "Well even though it's only brief, I can get some relief by engaging in this behavior." Unfortunately the anxiety always returns and the compulsive behavior is used again, causing a never-ending cycle.

If you have made mistakes, there is always another chance for you. You may have a fresh start any moment you choose, for this thing we call "failure" is not the falling down, but the staying down.

—Mary Pickford, actress and producer

If you were to try to stop going on social media for a day, you'd feel an increase in anxiety. If you suddenly decided you couldn't take it anymore and went on Instagram, your anxiety would suddenly go down. This is what reinforces the "obsessiveness" of checking social media all the time. So, if you think checking out social media is influencing your mood or making you more anxious, here's how you learn to break this habit.

MY PROFILE (UPDATE) (ACTIVITY)

CURRENT UPDATES:

JAN 20: 7:05 AM
BEFORE SCHOOL I GOT
TO POP FOUR REALLY
BIG JUICY ZITS

JAN 19: 1:37 AM
SCRUFFY HAD TO TAKE
A DUMP, LATE AT NIGHT.
AND IT WAS RAINING TOO.

Remember, when you try to stop checking social media, anxiety (and all emotions) will increase at first, but eventually they max out and start to go back down. If you engage in the behavior (checking social media) while the anxiety is still going up (before it reaches its peak), you teach yourself that you cannot handle the anxiety. To break this habit, hold off on social media, allow the anxiety to go up and up until it maxes out, and eventually notice the anxiety going back down. That's how you teach your brain that you can handle it. It'll be difficult the first few times, but like anything, you get better at it the more you try.

 DR. TOM'S TAKE

OFFLINE IS THE NEW LUXURY

Unfortunately, bullying is a horrible experience for some people as they grow up. And with the increase in technology, bullying has taken a natural course from being in your face to online, or both. However, it's not all bad news. While bullying continues to happen, there is more being done at schools, more programs to change attitudes of students, and continued AI development and research to help stop this from happening.

Bullying, like many topics Jon and I cover in this book, is too broad for us to thoroughly cover within one chapter. Our goal is to provide you with effective and easy-to-apply tips to help you in the moment. If bullying is happening to you on a regular basis, one of the most helpful things you can do for yourself (remember, you can do something about all things in your life) is to start researching bullying on your own. There are lots of great resources out there. Resources such as StompOutBullying.org and CyberBullying.org are great places to start.

It is important to note that some people in this world are genuinely dangerous. They do not care about being punished and likely will not change their behavior. If you think you are dealing with someone like this, contact an authority figure and share what is happening to you. You are supposed to feel safe, and there are professionals that can help.

WHY ME?

This is one of the most common questions I hear from teenagers and adults who are currently bullied or were bullied at some point in their lives: Is something inherently wrong or flawed in them, something that made them easy targets? Could their bullies see something in them that they can't see in themselves? Unfortunately, when you start thinking like this, you automatically assume that there is something wrong, flawed, or bad about you. Otherwise, they wouldn't pick on you, right? Because they don't do it to other people. If everyone were bullied, then it wouldn't feel so bad, so there must be something specific about you. And there is (more on this in a minute).

But it's not that you are bad or flawed. This is the most important thing to remember. At your core, you need to tell yourself that you are not a bad or broken person. If this seems too difficult to do, try to imagine what your bully could say to you that would make you feel better. I know this probably seems tough to do, but it's highly effective, so try.

What would you like them to say to you that would validate your pain and provide you with a sense of comfort (not revenge)? It could be something as simple as imagining them saying, "I'm sorry, it's not about you," or it can be much longer and more thought-out.

Whatever you decide you would like to hear from them is what you will have to say to yourself. You build self-esteem by providing a sense of calm and confidence for yourself when you feel defeated. Whatever you decide you'd like to hear from them, that is your coping phrase to help you recognize you are not whatever bad thing you think you might be. After coming up with this phrase, your job is to repeatedly recite it in your head whenever you start to believe you're at fault. If you feel like it's not working, try a new phrase that goes deeper emotionally in a soothing way. And remember to keep at it.

SO WHAT IS THE SPECIFIC THING MY BULLY NOTICES?

In general, what your bully notices is your behavior when you are bullied. They notice how you react, and your reaction feeds their taunting. Maybe you've tried not reacting a few times. But, overall, it's hard not to. There is a genuine fear when you're bullied of being hurt in some way, either physically or emotionally. Having this fear does not make you weak. We all have this fear because of how our brains are wired. Our long-ago, cave-dwelling ancestors were the ones that passed down these genes because being afraid kept them alive.

Being aware that your reaction feeds into a bully's motivation is important. This allows you to tell yourself ahead of time (like if you have the same class with the bully) to prepare yourself, stay calm, and not react. Remember: they can't play tug-of-war with you if you don't pick up the rope.

It would be easy to read the preceding and blame yourself. "If it's my reaction that's causing this, then it must be my fault." That's not true.

Just because your reaction can exacerbate the bullying does not mean it's your fault! You are not to blame. Sometimes, complicated situations, like bullying, happen because of complicated reasons. There's no way to know these things just by asking yourself why it's happening. That's why this book, professionals, and other resources are available. Because people cannot do this on their own. It's too difficult.

IMPORTANT TIPS WHEN YOU ARE BEING BULLIED

- Tell someone. You are not being a snitch by getting your parents or a teacher involved. Suffering in silence is the least helpful thing you can do for yourself. If everyone thinks you're having a good day, how is anything going to change?
- Recruit others to step in. Did you know that if other students step into a bullying situation and tell the bully to stop it works within 10 seconds more than half the time? If you're able, find other friends or peers ahead of time and talk about what you will do if someone starts to bully you or them. Making an agreement ahead of time can help in the heat of the moment. If it's possible, having someone that is popular or well liked step in on your behalf can improve the odds of this approach helping.

- Try not to react. Antibullying posters and assemblies aren't going to eliminate bullying. Do your best to remain as neutral as possible. If you show that you are feeling angry or afraid the bully will use this to keep taunting you. Every accomplishment starts with a decision to try.

- If you see them randomly, do not turn around and walk away. This will only let them know that you are afraid while encouraging their torments. It's best to continue walking on your path and appear unfazed. Don't express anything that would let them know what they're saying is bothering you. The less concerned you look, the worse they will appear to others.

- Develop an interest outside of school. Everyone has some type of interest or hobby they can focus on. Music, fitness, or art are all good areas to consider. Try to approach this interest with a long-term goal of steady improvement over time. You'll find with regular practice, you can get really good. This new skill can help improve the way you feel about yourself and often makes others see you in a new way. This is the concept of mastery.

- Remind yourself it's just the opinion of one, or a limited number of broken people. While this is the only world you know right now, the opinions of your bully do not represent the majority. When we don't have as much experience, it's easy to take what experiences we do have, globalize them, and say to ourselves "If nobody here likes me, then nobody else out there will like me either." Remember, life really starts after the age of 18 for most of us. That's when you get to go live where you want (being a good student can help with this) and work toward something you desire. You don't need to worry about being around the people from middle or high school after you graduate.

- Curb thoughts of revenge. The anger that comes with wanting revenge just makes you suffer when you're not being bullied. You're putting yourself in a no-win situation where you're tormented, even when you're by yourself. And, truthfully, you would not want to carry out these thoughts in real life. If you hurt someone badly, you'd eventually have deep regrets and you could end up in jail—where there are even more miserable bullies. Wanting to hurt someone comes from feeling deeply invalidated. Antibullying isn't bullying the bullies. Work on caring less about the bully while providing validation for yourself during these moments.

WAYS TO ALLEVIATE ANXIETY

17. Practice mindfulness. Root yourself in the present moment, accepting it without judgment and looking neither to the past nor the future. Mindfulness is a form of meditation and a key element of happiness.

18. Go for a walk or a hike, preferably in a park or nature setting. Being in nature is a fast remedy for anxiety.

19. Limit your time on social media. Since you can't control some of the asinine posts from "friends," you can limit your exposure.

20. Stop comparing yourself to others. Doing so is one of the quickest routes to unhappiness and stress. Take solace in knowing that you are right where you need to be at this moment. Your life and course are yours alone.

21. Use calming oils (aka aromatherapy) such as lavender. Consider using a small diffuser. It may seem trite and pointless, but it works well. Inhaling the aroma from the essential oils of flowers, bark, stems, leaves, and roots is widely believed to stimulate brain function and enhance psychological well-being.

22. Take a day trip. It could mean getting out of your typical surroundings to somewhere you enjoy, either alone or with a friend/loved one.

23. See how far you can stretch. Work to become more flexible. Anxiety typically has us in knots. Literally.

24. Go to the batting cages.

CHAPTER 4

FAMILY

A dysfunctional family is any family with more than one person in it.

—from *The Liars' Club* by Mary Karr

FREAKS OF NURTURE

Anxiety was a constant strain on my relationships with family members, mainly in how difficult it was for them to understand why I responded so differently to stimuli from anyone else. Much of it was due to misperceiving things people said and did while I used mental filters (a topic Dr. McDonagh and I will cover in Chapter 12). But my anxious behavior in general was confusing to family and anyone close to me.

Family aside, keep in mind that anxiety is a natural human condition that serves a healthy purpose. Your goal should be to keep it at a healthy and manageable level, not attempt to eliminate it entirely. My dad exhibits a few anxious traits, such as "hyper-collecting" (aka not discarding useless things) and attempting to control the unforeseeable, though he adamantly denies it and chastises me for saying so. As an adoptee, is my anxiety due to nature or nurture? I don't know. It doesn't matter. My chronic anxiety is due to an unfortunate mix of factors. Managing anxiety is my fate.

WHERE DID YOUR ANXIETY COME FROM?

Anxiety can certainly have genetic origins, biologically gifted from parent to child. Or, it can occur via "anxiety seed-planting," where a child's anxiety can proliferate at the hands of heavy parental control or through constant exposure. Some research indicates that people with certain personality traits are more vulnerable to anxiety. But it is likely a combination of contributing factors that lead to your particular anxiety, and you can't always identify the source or change tough circumstances that affect you. Other causes, such as negative self-talk and always telling yourself the worst will happen, can be avoided. How you became anxious does not affect what we do for you now, which is working to lessen it. It might be nice to know the roots of your anxiety; beyond that, it doesn't matter. In reality, the notion of genetic versus environmental contributors is complex and not easily understood. Your parents can have anxiety and/or depression while you never show a sign, or vice versa, where your parents are void of any mental disorders while you shotgun all sorts of neurosis.

> *Dysfunctional families have sired a number of pretty good actors.*
>
> —Gene Hackman, actor

The beauty of family is that they're the one group that accepts the real you at face value with no explanations needed. Your family receives the burden of your anxiety because they've known you the longest and are already privy to all your potential neurosis. Plus, they can't kick you out of the family tree.

A huge frustration for anxiety sufferers is that people couldn't identify anxiety if it were in a lineup or see it at all. They can see the irrational manifestations in all its various forms, but not the anxiety itself. An arrow to the head they would see. Anxiety—not so much. It has always felt unfair to suffer so much when the wounds are invisible. You can't see diabetes, leukemia, or unicorns either, but they're just as real.

I've always wondered what anxiety would look like if you could see it. I bet it's hideous.

THE ROLE OF FAMILY

Though it's highly preferred, don't expect your family to comprehend anxiety or how you feel. It's awesome if they do, but there's a good chance they won't. Most people without the bitter sting of anxiety have no idea how much you're suffering; they just look at you in cockeyed bewilderment. Moreover, try not to judge any lack of understanding. Just tell them how bleeding edge you are to have a sixth sense of hyper-vigilance that they lack. Support from family and friends is important to the recovery process, but it's not the cure, and you can get better despite anyone else. It might not be easy, but it's going to be worth it.

At a minimum, however, family members will likely require some coaching on things not to say to you regarding anxiety, such as the following nuggets often dispensed by friends and loved ones.

THINGS NOT TO SAY TO THE ANXIETY SUFFERER

- "Can't you just calm down?!"
- "It's just a thought."
- "Don't sweat the small stuff."
- "Everything will be okay."
- "Oh, I get it—I'm stressed too. I know how you feel."
- "It's not a big deal."
- "It's all in your head."
- "It could be so much worse."
- "Just move on!"
- "Are you just gonna sit there and mope?"
- "Cheer up!"
- "Smile!"

- "You're overreacting/too sensitive/too emotional."
- "Try not to think about it."
- "Don't be so pessimistic."
- "You just need to drink/smoke/take meds."
- "Have you tried running/meditation/vitamins/yoga?"
- "You have so much to be happy about."
- "What do you have to be anxious about?"
- "Dude, chill."
- "Why are you freaking out?"
- "You look really tired."
- "At least there's nothing physically wrong with you."
- "Stop dwelling."
- "What's wrong with you?"
- "Why don't you just pop a Xanax?"
- "There are people in this world with real problems."
- "You worry too much."
- "You should try to be more positive."
- "Anxiety isn't a real thing."

It's tough to take when loved ones trivialize your pain due to a lack of understanding. Family and friends might comprehend getting nervous at times, but they often can't grasp that going to a crowded amusement park, concert, or party can feel like a crippling act of self-sabotage and doom rather than fun. My brother, for example, never understood my anxiety. He still doesn't. He just thinks I'm mis-wired or a paste-eater. I've repeatedly tried to explain to him what and how I feel, to no avail. He tells me, "Dude, it's just a thought" or "You need a new therapist." If only he could see the mind-chewing anxiety monster, then he'd believe. God bless him—he's jealous of my superpowers to leap to conclusions or predict worst-case scenarios. A good way of thinking of certain people, loved ones included, is as a dry well. You can keep going back for a drink while thirsty, but you'll never get any water. I don't love family members any less for not understanding me, especially my parents who, despite not fully understanding my anxiety, do their best to support me. Your anxiety and imperfections are what make you unique. If we were all perfect, we'd all be the same. No thank you. Look, if someone takes issue with your anxiety, blood related or not, that's their problem, not yours. You can't choose family, but you can always choose yourself.

In absence of knowing better, family might push you into doing things that make you feel worse, simply because they believe your fears are unfounded. Consider the humble elevator, for example. My single greatest fear in life was this boxcar to hell. I'd just as soon ride a salt mine elevator than any standard American office version. I still hate them and take stairs whenever possible, which is anything under 800 floors. My mom wrongly assumed that dragging me into elevators to regularly ride them would "cure" my aversion, which included screaming, outright panic, tears, and begging for my life.

I had to get over elevator claustrophobia at my own pace by exposing myself to them little by little in buildings I deemed were up to code. I would choose to ride them as often as tolerable, but only if they appeared ride-worthy, had a current inspection certificate posted, and contained other riders so I wouldn't die alone. Other people weren't aware of my maniacal anxiety unless the elevator did something odd, which was about 15 percent of the time. Mechanical oddities included pausing to open or trying to sever limbs with the doors; jolting or bumping; making any sound construed as dicey; or playing a Muzak system of foreboding songs that presaged terror.

Whatever your fears, worries, and anxieties—they are real. But don't mistake real with accurate or factual. What you feel is absolutely measurable. But why you feel what you feel should be questioned and challenged. I've now ridden thousands of elevators worldwide, including one with MC Hammer, and have yet to be killed, mutilated, or wear Hammer pants. I cannot overstate that thoughts and feelings do not equal facts, just as an anxiety attack can make you feel like you're having a heart attack when you're not. The pain and angst are real, but you are not in cardiac arrest.

HOW TO MANAGE FAMILY RELATIONSHIPS

"You're only happy when you're miserable." This is the worst thing my dad ever said to me, though he meant no harm. There are many things wrong with this statement directed toward anyone with a mental disorder. But I'll only cover the most pertinent. No mental disorder is a choice. And I don't know anyone who wants to be miserable. If given the choice, I would have chosen to be obnoxiously joyous. There were decisive reasons for my anxiety disorder, none of which had anything to do with my consent.

At the time my dad voiced this statement, I had little coping ability to manage my anxiety. I didn't even know what was wrong with me, let alone how to take steps to feel better. If you're outwardly suffering from anxiety, it's likely because you don't know how to un-suffer from it. Don't let anyone make you feel guilty for feeling bad. That's like blaming someone for having allergies or being an aardvark.

Conversely, the most helpful thing said to me regarding my anxiety didn't come from a family member, but from a doctor. Hospitalized for an anxiety attack, I told the ER doc about my current state of mind, and she looked at me compassionately and simply stated, "I am so sorry. That must be really tough to deal with." It wasn't advice; it was simple acknowledgment of my pain. I felt her empathy reach my core, because it was real. And though she didn't understand it or know exactly what I was feeling, her attentiveness and extension of care was just what I needed.

Anxiety is rooted in irrational fears. So being told that you're ridiculous, a hypochondriac, or insane is counterproductive. It's perfectly okay to tell loved ones that it's not their responsibility to fix you, but to show care and help where it makes sense. Oftentimes, the most effective response from family is basic compassion and offering to be with you through your trials. The range of family support to your anxiety runs the full spectrum, from unsupportive or understanding to relentless doting in attempts to ease your pain, and everything in between. Be prepared for anything, while, hopefully, optimistic for love and support. What's important to share with family is that they don't need to know exactly how you feel. What's vital is that they show compassion and do their best to support you. That's it.

SOMETIMES FAMILY SUCKS

I recall suffering from anxiety as a kid and my mom explicitly telling me not to let certain relatives know what was wrong with me. I was to hide my "condition." I asked her why, and she replied, "They won't understand, and they'll judge you for it." I thought, "What asshats!"

Sadly, she was right. In the absence of understanding, some people, family included, will label you as damaged/strange/screwed up, etc., due to their own ignorance. Those same relatives and loved ones who once wondered about me now sit front row to my comeback. But I did it for me, not them. I relegated many of them to the annals of family history.

My next step was to find the smallest positive and build myself up from there. You simply don't need such people in your life. The greatest vindication to anything or anyone is happiness. You don't have to write a book, attain a certain title, or be the greatest anything but the happiest version of you possible. Anything beyond that is gravy. There are endless ways to channel your anxiety into greatness, whether it's academic success, athleticism, acting, volunteerism, or music and the arts. You alone are the master of your fate.

FIND THE PLUS SIGN AND BUILD FROM THERE

One way to become enthusiastic is to look for the plus sign. To make progress in any difficult situation, you have to start with what's right about it and build on that.
—Norman Vincent Peale, author of *The Power of Positive Thinking*

Anxiety can make doing certain things feel impossible. Even a simple decision can become "paralysis by analysis." This is how I am with the average restaurant menu. The more options available, the more likely I am to never make a decision, only to end up with "entrée envy" once my anxiety-ridden food choice arrives at the table. In the worst instances of anxiety, I would fry-out or short-circuit like a blender full of gravel left on purée until it starts smoking. Try to be Teflon, not Velcro.

Life isn't always pretty. It's often a process of overcoming and solving problems. This is how you test and develop your mettle and spiritual muscle. By rising to meet life's challenges, you become great—not in spite of, but because of your problems. When facing an obstacle, use it to create a positive result. Let your problems bring out your greatness. Don't loathe the problems you have; love them for the gifts they will impart. And rather than wish or pray for a life that is problem-free, ask for one that is solution-full.

Dear brothers and sisters, when troubles of any kind come your way, consider it an opportunity for great joy. For you know that when your faith is tested, your endurance has a chance to grow. So let it grow, for when your endurance is fully developed, you will be perfect and complete, needing nothing.
—James 1:2–4

I frequently recite the simple phrase, "Not my pigs, not my farm" whenever my anxiety is trying to pull me into something. Try saying it aloud. It works by reminding you to avoid letting something external dictate my agenda in a negative direction.

Remember, you don't have to accept every invite anxiety offers you.

DR. TOM'S TAKE

ANXIETY DOESN'T FALL FAR FROM THE TREE

When working with you and anxiety, if Jon and I only talked about you, we'd miss out on a big portion of your life. This is because you, as an individual, do not exist in a vacuum. You come across different types of people during your day: your classmates, your teachers, coaches, sometimes your dentist, maybe a caseworker, and of course, the big one: your family.

Families have a huge impact on how we feel about ourselves, how we approach our day, and how we interact with other people. So, more than you might want to admit, your family life is important when it comes to reducing your anxiety, which, if you think about it, makes sense. How you interact with your family sets the foundation for how you interact with other people. Our families teach us, in part, how we are seen by others and how to respond to other people.

For example, if you grow up in a household where everyone respects each other (most of the time … this is family, after all) and listens to each other's opinions, then you would expect other people to do the same. On the flip side, if you grow up in a home where this doesn't happen, or you always receive mixed messages, then you might feel like you're walking on eggshells all the time. It's possible that you'll be anxious without even realizing it!

Now, I want to be clear about something. The casual reader might look at the above paragraph and use it as ammunition to blame family for their problems. Allow me to gently put an end to that thought. This is not a chance for you to blame your family. Nor is this an opportunity for you to look at your family and say, "You are the reason I am this way!" That is not what I am saying. (Plus, just as a general rule, blaming is never helpful for any situation.) What I am saying is you interact with your family a lot, and sometimes, working with family issues will help to reduce your anxiety.

So, let's talk about some family dynamics (ways family members interact with each other) that can contribute to anxiety. We'll talk about three of the biggest issues (from Murray Bowen, MD), then we'll talk about what to do with them.

Nerd Fact: Family therapy theories have many "founders," but some important people to know are Murray Bowen, Jay Haley, and a group of scientists who founded the Milan school of family therapy.

POTENTIAL PROBLEM 1: "DIFFERENTIATION OF SELF"

Don't let the preceding phrase scare you! It just means "how you grow up into an older person." When you say things like "Mom/Dad, I don't need your help," that is you "differentiating yourself." The ability to brush your own teeth and dress yourself, becoming less dependent on your caretakers, is an example. So is being able to drive your younger sibling to soccer practice after school. Basically, it's the things you do as you get older that define you as acting more like an adult.

Here's the reason why having problems with this can be an issue. If you don't gradually learn to depend on yourself, it can create anxiety because you may then depend too much on other people for approval and acceptance. What does this look like? You tend to take on the emotions or problems of others (like your family) as your own all the time. You always tend to feel like it was your fault that someone else felt badly. So to prevent yourself from feeling like it's your fault, you do what other people want you to do, all the time, and never say what you want. If this is often happening to you, you're going to feel anxiety. It's not your fault, it's just the way we are wired in our brains. Anyone who regularly does this would feel the exact same way.

To be fair, we all do things at times to get along with other people. So it's important to recognize the difference between doing something because you are a part of a family and that's just what you have to do in the moment, and never saying what you want.

POTENTIAL PROBLEM 2: "TRIANGLES"

Triangles just mean the way three people (think of your family) interact with each other. In families, there are more than two people involved. Even in single-child homes with one parent, there is typically another person involved in some way, be it a teacher, relative, neighbor, etc.

An example of a triangle would be you, your sibling, and a parent. But in your life, you interact with more than two people. Believe it or not, you have multiple relationships with other people in your life, so we call these "interlocking triangles." For example, you, your sibling, and one of your parents can create one triangle. But another triangle can have you, your sibling, and your other parent. The overlap with your parents creates the "interlocking triangle."

Family relationships are viewed as these triangles because it's how people naturally divide up to balance the stress of life. When it's just two people, the stress of life is too much and people will argue. So we pull in a third person to create some stability. This isn't something we are aware we are doing; it just happens, without us even realizing it.

The problem with these triangles is that during times of stress, two of the people will become closer and make the third person feel like an outsider. So what does the outsider do? They don't want to feel left out, so they work hard at trying to get closer to one of the insiders. Sometimes this works, sometimes it doesn't. But what happens is that at least one person is left feeling like they are on the outside.

Feeling like you are on the outside creates problems. Ever hear the phrase "the black sheep of the family"? That's what this is—one person feeling left out. Sometimes it's obvious who is on the outside, and sometimes it's much more subtle. But being on the outside and transitioning between the inside and outside positions can trigger anxiety issues.

POTENTIAL PROBLEM 3: "EMOTIONAL CUTOFF"

Sometimes people cope with problems in their family by limiting contact or communication with them as much as possible. When we withhold our love for others, we are emotionally cutting them off.

An example of this is when a teenager is upset with their parents and refuses to say anything to them for a period of time. The teenager feels that by refusing to say anything, they are gaining control of the situation. This might feel good in the short term, but creates issues over time as they never learn how to express difficult thoughts and emotions. This is particularly problematic if it becomes a pattern. The ability to express difficult emotions effectively is one of the most important skills to learn as a teenager.

Alternatively, parents are also capable of withholding affection if they feel hurt. This is also something to avoid, as it can cause a range of issues for the child, such as anxiety, guilt, or anger.

More common emotional cutoff behavior in families consists of "unmentionable topics." Avoiding specific issues is a way for families to reduce the tension in the home, but it teaches everyone that you do not have the ability to solve problems. The solution is to act like it's not there. This is essentially avoidance, and the more you avoid something, the more stress you will feel.

Let's start the process right now.

Create a Family Tree

Remember, you do not live in an empty space. You are who you are in large part because of the family in which you are raised. And, just like you, your parents and grandparents were raised in families that influenced them as well.

In an effort to promote family communication and discuss these issues, with at least one of your parents or caretakers, create a family tree. (FYI: If you are adopted this absolutely applies to your adopted family. You live with them and they influence you every day.)

On a large sheet of paper, starting on the left and going from oldest to youngest, include your grandparents, their siblings, and whom they married. Then move down and fill in all of your grandparents' children (your parents as well as your aunts and uncles). Be sure to include the people your aunts/uncles married. Then move down one last time and fill in the children of your parents (you and your siblings!) as well as the children of your aunts/uncles (your cousins).

On a separate sheet of paper, for each name, write down that person's key life events and how your parents feel that person influenced them. Also include how you think that person influenced you. Try to use this as a way to see that you are part of a bigger picture, and one that goes back generations. Hopefully, this creates an opportunity for you and your family to talk about family patterns and see if there is anything you want to change.

Family 69

25. Call your grandparents or go talk to an older neighbor. Ask them about their childhood.

26. Think of a happy moment in your life and dwell on it for a bit.

27. Do your laundry (it's actually relaxing!), or unload the dishwasher/help clean the dishes.

28. Read a book or magazine.

29. Put your hand on whatever object is in front of you. Write down as many different words as you can to describe what that object feels like under your hand.

30. Listen to music you love. It's simple and effective.

31. Go on a bike ride.

32. Learn how to say something very weird in a different language (e.g., "I don't like to eat soup with my tweed vest on" or "Cold feet make me think slowly").

CHAPTER 5

SCHOOL ANXIETY

The average teenager has the same level of anxiety as a
psychiatric patient in the early 1950s.

—Dr. Robert Leahy

HOW I GOT AN "A" IN ANXIETY

A growing problem facing teenagers today, anxiety is the most common
mental illness in the US. As Dr. McDonagh explains later in "How Not
to Get an 'A' in Anxiety," feeling stress about school is normal, even
though it feels like something you don't have control over. I crushed
an impressive amount of anxiety into one kid. But school provided
plentiful distractions ranging from sports and clubs to abundant social
and sexual awkwardness. Despite my stated dislike of academics, the
institution of formal education required that I be present at the same
time and place each day and at least slightly focused for seven hours
straight. This was the order from the state of California, but not how it
always played out for me. My unregulated anxiety had its own rogue

agenda. At this life stage, my brain was still mostly useless at responding to all the nervous stimuli.

Anxiety was a new and unwelcome aspect of my teenage life, resulting in high school years peppered with trouble, on-campus detention, and long periods of restriction at home. House arrest was the single worst penance for me. I was like a caged spider monkey, bouncing from carpet to ceiling and wall to wall. The upside was learning early on that I'd never survive within a county or state penal system. This would prove valuable later, when my impulsivity increased. If I couldn't do without sugar and MTV for a week, I'd never survive juvie.

I didn't know what was wrong with me or how to feel better, and much of my anguish resulted in cutting. It was my flawed belief that I should be punished for feeling so bad. This fuzzy logic was worsened by being an awful cutter. I chose prominent locations like my face and forearms, which drew attention from my keen parents since I looked like a feral cat herder whose shepherding tool was his face. I chose these body parts because that's what I felt like cutting. That's the wisdom of cutting: if I couldn't cut the anxiety, I would cut sensitive places as if the anxiety lived there. It's particularly sad that I intentionally hurt myself for feeling so bad. Cutting myself because of painful anxiety made sense like hammering my own genitals with a mallet after a bike accident makes sense.

I wasn't sure why I cut, beyond a feeling of release or as a harmful coping mechanism. "The vast majority of kids who cut themselves do so as an emotion-regulation strategy, and unfortunately, it works, which is why it's so hard to get them to stop," explains Dr. Michael Hollander, author and director of training and consultations for the 3East dialectical behavioral therapy program at McLean Hospital in Belmont, Massachusetts. "Kids who cut themselves are either jumping out of their skin and use self-injury to calm themselves down, or are numb and empty and use self-injury to feel something. A small percentage use it for avoidance, to create a distraction, and an even smaller percentage use it to get attention. Some, a very small group of kids, use it to punish themselves."

There are complications to cutting and self-injury to consider. These include worsening feelings of shame, guilt, and low self-esteem; infection; permanent scars or disfigurement; severe and possibly fatal injury; and worsening of underlying issues and disorders if not adequately treated.

Why so much teen angst? What did I have to be so anxious about as a Little League pitcher and part-time school crossing guard? I had no idea. I still don't. That's how life works; it's seldom fair. How I learned to manage anxiety is where the sweet spot lies for me and for you. There are anxiety-contributing factors in every situation where the teenage brain is not as experienced in handling the bewilderment of anxiety. In general, the teen years are made up of a steady deluge of new anxiety-inducing provocations, including SATs, self-image, sex, driving, how to skillfully mask acne, or how to look cool carrying a book on anxiety.

Anxiety happens when you think you have to figure everything out. You don't.

When I wasn't cutting, I coped with anxiety by not coping. Instead, I ignored it and became irritable, hating things and people. This often meant starting fights, mostly with my older brother during school lunches, when he would pummel me like a skinny-jeaned Abercrombie mannequin in front of our peers. I repeatedly pledged that his demise would come the next time we grappled at high noon. I somehow attained an enviable social status that included being voted "Campus Clown" and (far less desirable) "Campus Mouth," accolades my parents never appreciated as they pinned their hopes on "Most Likely to Succeed" or even "Least Problematic" or "Middle-of-the-Packer."

Due to my regular, anxiety-based capers, upon graduation, the school mailed a formal letter to my house declaring me permanently banned from entering campus again.

If the array of self-inflicted wounds weren't a roadmap to my anxiety, the panic attacks that had me fist-pounding my chest for enough air were. At first, the panic attacks appeared as asthma. But when my mom inquired about my symptoms and I immediately shouted my worries about grades, snipers, my pitching arm, nuclear proliferation in Eastern Europe, a complete lack of acceptable dance moves for the upcoming prom, and what I perceived as a pending invasion by the Russian military, she wished it were only asthma. I was suffering from something far more insidious and expensive.

A panic attack (the clinical term for an anxiety attack) is the abrupt onset of intense fear or discomfort that reaches a peak within minutes and includes at least four of the following symptoms:

- Palpitations, pounding heart, or accelerated heart rate.
- Sweating.
- Trembling or shaking.
- Sensations of shortness of breath or smothering.
- Feelings of choking.
- Chest pain or discomfort.
- Nausea or abdominal distress.
- Feeling dizzy, unsteady, lightheaded, or faint.
- Chills or heat sensations.
- Paresthesia (numbness or tingling sensations).
- Derealization (feelings of unreality) or depersonalization (being detached from oneself).
- Fear of losing control or "going crazy."
- Fear of dying.

Are You Going Insane?

When anxiety's at its worst, you may feel you're losing your mind. It's a real and common experience for many people with anxiety and panic attacks. But the feeling that you're going crazy is the anxiety itself. Oftentimes, the only reason I knew I wasn't actually going insane was because I was able to cognitively process the question of whether or not I was going crazy. If you're actually going insane, you typically won't have the presence of mind to know.

Are you going insane? No. You can't suddenly go nuts, despite how you feel. Panic attacks can certainly make you feel like you're losing it or your mind is somehow failing you. It's not. Anxiety is not the same as a true psychotic episode.

Anxiety can make you feel isolated as you believe you're the only one going through it. I thought I was a wuss for suffering panic attacks and might have gone on thinking so had it not been for our high school football quarterback, Chris, a menacing athlete in both size and reputation. Even his face heaved with muscle. On a regular visit to the principal's office one afternoon, I spotted him lying on his back in the nurse's station, dazed and generally unresponsive. His girlfriend was in the hall outside the room, and when she saw my shock at seeing him so vulnerable, she plainly stated, "OMG ... He's having one of those anxiety attacks. Whatever." To see our campus titan reduced to a soft heap of sad butter by an invisible and stealth cerebral assassin was awe-inspiring to me. If the captain of our football team could be crippled by an anxiety attack, then perhaps I had seen firsthand the psychological kryptonite and great equalizer of us all! Clearly no one was immune.

Never be afraid to try. Remember, amateurs built the Ark, professionals built the Titanic.

Once my parents were aware of my affliction, I landed in weekly talk therapy sessions with a licensed clinical social worker (LCSW) who asked lots of questions as I shared my anxiety-ridden views on school, geopolitics, friends, and terrorists, and my fears about a resurgence of diphtheria, rickets, or boy bands. Most of what I shared, no teen should have on their worry radar. I don't know where I developed so much worry and anxiety—probably from CNN. But I can say with conviction and regret that I missed most of my teenage years on pointless fears and anxieties. Looking back, not one of my main apprehensions came to pass. The things that filled my worry well were the least likely to actually occur. The Russian infantry didn't attack, and I never got anything worse than mononucleosis. But the boy band thing happened.

My case was not at all unusual. In a study conducted by Dr. Robert Leahy, author and editor of 23 books, including *The Worry Cure*, 85 percent of what subjects worried about never occurred. And of the remaining 15 percent that did materialize, 79 percent of study subjects discovered they could handle the difficulty better than expected.

Despite counseling and the resulting medications I took for anxiety and insomnia, I was one toxic thought wad away from panic attacks and mental paralysis. Medicine treated the physical symptoms and manifestations of anxiety, but never the underlying causes.

Unfortunately, as a member of a huge HMO, I simply did not receive enough face time with any therapist to learn the necessary skills that Dr. McDonagh and I teach in this book. Instead, I was in long-term triage. Let my case be an incentive for getting your own anxiety under control now. You don't have to suffer the way I did, or for nearly as long. No one knew the depth of my suffering because I never divulged just how anxious I felt from day to day. I wasn't sure how to put a descriptor on how I truly felt.

It's accurate to say that it was during my teen years that I completely botched getting anxiety under control. I remained retroactive rather than proactive, always responding after the fact rather than learning the skills to lessen or eliminate the anxiety altogether. I was far from the anxiety subduer I am today—and that you, too, can be.

> *Nobody realizes that some people expend tremendous amounts of energy merely to be normal.*
>
> —Albert Camus

For teens with anxiety, it may seem like the key objective during your school years is to remain functional while keeping up appearances, lest anyone judge you for lacking in some way. This was, at least, my personal experience in a competitive academic environment. I was on antianxiety pills by day and sleep medication by night. I never felt right while consistently drugged. Too often, pills are the go-to treatment prescribed to teens as a fast track to relief. I will never dispute that medication has its time and place; but I was rarely involved in such discussions. I just opened up and swallowed morning and night. What's more impactful and sustaining than meds? Skills! Skills! Skills! I cannot overemphasize the importance of developing simple anxiety-countering aids to dramatically lessen your angst to surprisingly manageable levels. The only side effects to skills usage are mastery, self-reliance, and feeling better! And, you can't drink, pop, huff, or smoke that.

When you are living with anxiety, an overriding theme of high school is emotional fatigue. It can be draining to keep up appearances while limiting trouble to a minimum and graduating with decent grades. In my case, for example, I successfully managed most homework but made everything harder than it was. I required outside tutoring, particularly in math, a subject I hated on looks alone, with all those random numbers and symbols demanding that I provide some absurd reply.

Anxiety is worsened by stress related to grades, exams, class ranking, and college prep, and I worried extensively about all of these things.

I discovered that the most unlikely aspects can benefit an anxiety-ridden lifestyle. For me, these consisted of a fixed bedtime, two German shepherds, and three best friends living on my street. Daily dog walks with my best buds and their family dogs each evening were extraordinarily soothing to my well-being.

"Idle time often leads to overthinking and over-magnifying. In other words, if you aren't stimulated or busy, you're apt to zero in on trivial things and obsess over them," says John Tsilimparis, MFT, director of the Anxiety and Panic Disorder Center of Los Angeles. Having a plan for each day to include productivity, pleasure, and exercise goals is important. Anxiety thrives where there is a lack of structure.

> *It isn't stress that makes us fall—it's how we respond to stressful events.*
>
> —Wayde Goodall

Though you may not realize it now, the more activities you are exposed to—whether of your own accord or that of your parent(s)—the better. The exposure to various things will provide the best chance at discovering things you enjoy, and possibly excel in, later. For example, my mother insisted that I practice writing cursive for hours on end. At the time, it felt like just another rote task. It wasn't until years later that I realized how much I enjoyed not just writing, but the act of creating the letters on the page. I wish this worked for the piano lessons. But you will never know the things you most enjoy unless you're exposed to them, even if it's against your own volition. Turns out that parents are often smarter than we think. My mom had no idea that when she assigned all that writing, she was honing my writing career. Not only was she helping me counter my anxiety through structure, but she was ensuring I'd have enough skills to get out of her hair one day. Well played, Mom.

> *I am stronger than I think.*
>
> —You

DR. TOM'S TAKE

HOW NOT TO GET AN "A" IN ANXIETY

Feeling stress about school is normal for any student. We all have it in some form or another. Producer and writer Judd Apatow is aptly quoted as saying, "College is the reward for high school." So it's okay that you're feeling overwhelmed about school. It makes you normal! Welcome to the club.

Keep in mind, since you spend so much of your life in those academic buildings, it makes sense that a large part of your mind is also focused there. Aside from your actual home, school is likely the place you spend most of your time, and with the exact same people. Expectations are placed upon you every day. This, like most things, can be a bad thing if there's too much keeping the stressed-out mind busy, such as friends, other people in your school, teachers liking you, teachers not liking you, sports, clubs, homework, and so much more. If you were seeking a recipe for anxiety, this would be it! And, if reading that makes you feel more nervous, do not fret. Again, you are not alone in your worries. Just ask Jon.

So let's talk about what you can actually do about some of this school anxiety. When professionals want to help someone make their anxiety go away, they help the person break their anxiety down into three specific areas: thoughts, behaviors, and physical symptoms.

We do this because anxiety often feels like something we don't have control over, as though it happens to us. And because we feel it's something that happens to us, we feel like it's our fault that we feel this way.

For example, someone who feels like experiencing anxiety is their fault might say to themselves, "I'm so weak," "What's wrong with me?" or "Why can't I stop thinking/feeling like this?!" These crushing thoughts are examples of self-blame. This is normal, and we all do it naturally. But just because you think something does not make it true.

Blaming yourself for experiencing anxiety is like blaming yourself for getting the flu. It's not a personal thing, it's a medical thing. And gaining control by organizing your symptoms into thoughts, behaviors, and physical symptoms is the beginning of anxiety treatment.

By starting the process of organizing your anxiety into these three categories, you stop feeling like anxiety has control over you because there are things you can do. Do not forget this, because it's powerful. This is how you start to change.

Let's begin the process right now!

Identifying Your Thoughts, Behaviors, and Physical Symptoms

1. Start with your thoughts about school. Write down the top 10 worry thoughts. If you can't come up with 10, not a problem! If you can come up with more, I say stop at 10 because it's more important to work with the most common thoughts. You don't need to get every random thought out there. Ten is more than enough.

2. Now, list the top 10 behaviors you do when you are anxious at school. Identify what it is that you actually do when you are feeling anxious, worried, or nervous at school. This could be looking at your phone, walking away, biting your nails, talking rapidly, etc. There is no wrong answer. You simply want a list of school-related anxiety behaviors. Again, stop at 10.

3. Now, identify your physical symptoms. When you start to feel anxious, nervous, or worried at school, what physical symptoms do you experience? Examples might include an increase in your heartbeat, starting to sweat, feeling numbness in your face or body, getting hot or cold flashes, getting tunnel vision, or any other physical sensations. Again, there are no wrong answers! If it's happening to you, it's important to note. List as many as you are able. If you go beyond 10, that's fine. Some people do, some don't.

33. Get organized. The first things people tend to avoid when anxiety escalates are routine obligations. Clean your room, organize your closet, write that research paper, etc. Getting something done that's been on your back is extremely gratifying.

34. Know and accept that your anxiety will pass. Anxiety ebbs and flows. Accept it as it waxes and wanes over and through you. Remember, accepting it robs it of its power over you.

35. Go outside, find a bird, and try to identify it. There are some cool apps that identify bird sounds. They can even sing and communicate back to the birds for full-on ornithological banter!

36. Stare gently at a spot on the floor for five minutes. Observe what happens to your vision and thoughts.

37. Splash cold water on your face.

38. Write a list of your skills and strengths. You are extremely competent, but anxiety can rob you of feelings of self-competency. Take some time to write down as many of your strengths as you can. Keep adding to the list over time, and reread regularly.

39. Remind yourself that you are doing the best you can for where you are in this moment. Because that's the truth.

40. Doodle or sketch.

CHAPTER 6

DATING, SEX, AND POPULARITY

DO YOU LIKE ME? DO YOU? HOW 'BOUT NOW?

My parents tried to avoid the prepubescent sex talk entirely by giving me an odd paperback titled *Boys and Sex*, then asking later if I had read it. I don't know if they were lazy or just hated talking to me. If it wasn't a comic book or the back of a cereal box, I didn't read it. Fortunately, the next option I had to learn about sex was outdated sex education films played in elementary school Sex Ed class. But we all laughed through the awkward narration and scripted intimacy.

> *I've been single for a while, and I have to say it's going very well. Like ... it's working out. I think I'm the one.*

In addition to offering the sex education book, my dad also advised me never to get hung up on a girl, which I epically failed at. Valerie was her name, and she threw me for a loop. In this chapter, Dr. McDonagh and I will discuss what my parents never talked about: how to handle the anxieties of dating.

RELATIONSHIP OBSESSIVE COMPULSIVE DISORDER

The form of anxiety that comes with liking someone is so common that it has its own acronym: ROCD (relationship obsessive compulsive disorder). ROCD is much like any other form of OCD where one experiences distressing and undesired thoughts about the state and traits of their relationship. Obsessions in ROCD include ruminations regarding a partner's appropriateness as a mate, overall level of attractiveness, sexual desirability, or long-term compatibility. With ROCD, obsessions usually fall into one of two categories: (1) Questioning whether you love your partner, or (2) Wondering whether your partner loves you. Instead of finding good in their partner, ROCD sufferers are constantly focused on their shortcomings to prove the relationship is fundamentally broken. The doubts and indecisions are never-ending, and OCD is often not identified as the culprit.

Common obsessive ROCD thoughts include:

- Do I really love him/her?
- What if he/she is not the one?
- Am I settling?
- If I don't think about my partner for periods of time, do I really love him/her?
- If I don't feel like being intimate, does it mean I'm not attracted to my partner?
- I notice other attractive guys/girls; am I in the wrong relationship?
- I enjoy time alone. Does this mean I'm not really in love with my partner?
- I can imagine cheating on my partner, so I must secretly want to be with someone else.
- I can't stop fixating on his/her flaws regarding appearance or character.

ROCD is real, and you are not alone. The more you like the person, the more anxiety/ROCD you're likely to feel. Handle these anxious thoughts as you would any anxiety-related thoughts: Let them pass over and through you, holding onto nothing while accepting them as what they are—anxiety. The best treatment for ROCD is the same as management of OCD. The goal of OCD or ROCD treatment is to help you to develop a greater tolerance for ambiguity or troublesome thoughts.

In the past, I left many opportunities on the table with regard to meeting women, until the day I ran into a buddy at an outdoor country concert. I will call him "Bryan." As I feigned interest in whatever Bryan was saying, I interrupted him to point out a stunning blonde 10 yards away. While I was busy convincing myself that she had a boyfriend and was way out of my league, Bryan was already introducing himself to her. Since the beautiful girl had a cute friend with her, I opted to be a good wingman and walk over. Much to my awe, Bryan was soon entering the blonde's number into his phone. Again, I convinced myself of another falsehood: that she had given him a fake number. A few days later, I learned I was wrong on this account when Bryan called to tell me about his amazing date with her. I was beside myself with resentment. In this life-changing moment, I decided it was far better to heal from the sting of quick, potential humiliation than to spend days regretting inaction. No matter how amazing you are, not every single person of interest can like you back. You may not be the person everyone wants, and that's far better than being the one everyone's had.

THE SWEET BLISS OF PERSONAL BOUNDARIES

Personal boundaries = Respect for self. And a lack of boundaries invites a lack of respect. People only treat you the way you allow them to. You cannot force someone to respect you, but you can always prevent someone from disrespecting you. If someone truly wants to be in your life, they will respect your boundaries. End of story. If not, they're doing you a favor by going away.

To greatly reduce your odds of dating the wrong person, there is one commonly overlooked tool to implement before getting involved: personal property lines (aka boundaries). It's never too late to leverage the power of boundaries. When it comes to boundaries, you can learn to use them now or later, but the sooner the better. For the anxiety-prone, you don't have to date someone for long to become entangled with them. Here's a likely scenario: You don't know how it happened. You used to be so autonomous and "master of your domain." Now, you're clutching your chest because it feels like you can't breathe without them. Seems odd, right? I mean, you had an entire life before that pivotal day you met. So why does it suddenly feel like you can't make a sandwich without them?

Don't search for your other half. You're not a half.

Impenetrable personal boundaries guard us from dating ills. They're like invisible force fields that repel bullshit, douchebags, emotional abusers, and the undateable, and no one should risk dating without them. You wear a jacket when it's cold and a helmet when you ride, right? Yet so few of us adorn ourselves with interpersonal boundaries to protect the very thing that keeps us alive: our hearts! The notion of blindly investing your heart and feelings into any relationship sans boundaries should horrify you. Doing so is an open invitation to opportunists to have their way with you and your emotional well-being.

> *Before you diagnose yourself with depression or low self-esteem, first make sure that you are not, in fact, just surrounded by assholes.*
>
> —Unknown

Boundaries can prevent you from weeks, months, or years of anguish that can occur when you allow the wrong people into your life. Boundaries also prevent enmeshment. At the most basic level, enmeshment is a concept where your life becomes blurred with that of another. In this scenario, you don't know where you end and they begin. Whereas a healthy relationship consists of two whole entities that love and support one another while remaining complete on their own.

Enmeshment is "½ + ½ = 1." Another person does not actually complete you. You're complete on your own.

You're Complete on Your Own

1. You never want to complete anyone, or vice versa. A fence post that leans on another post makes a bad fence.
2. If, for whatever reason, the relationship ends, you will need to be a complete entity again. So why not remain one in the first place?

Establishing boundaries strengthens resolve and helps to rebuild self-esteem following a bad breakup. Creating them will directly contribute to the healing process while (bonus!) preventing you from relapsing back toward your ex. It gets even better. Establishing boundaries will actually protect you in regard to all of your interpersonal relationships, whether it's a matter of the heart, familial relationship, or work association, keeping tyrannical colleagues and managers from taking advantage of you or stealing your sandwiches and pens.

If I sound pragmatic or unemotional about this, I'm not. On the contrary, I am a huge proponent of healthy people and relationships that go the distance. Enmeshment counters this. I like to think of personal boundaries as a perimeter around the heart, and not the cute white picket fence you might be envisioning, but an impenetrable, tall, black iron-wrought fence with sharp points that only a ninja eunuch would consider scaling. This is precisely how your personal boundaries should work, where the only dates allowed entry are those who meet your predefined requirements that espouse who you are and reflect what you want in your life. Your individual requirements will vary but may include things like non-smoking/drinking, college-minded, spiritual/religious, or vegetarian/prefers food that craps on a vegetarian's food.

These are also the overlooked characteristics typically identified as red flags later when people contact us at State of Anxiety following a bad breakup. It's quite common for sufferers to write, "There were all these red flags early on, but I ignored them." What if you didn't ignore them? What if you screened for them at your "property line"? Always heed your intuition. Even better, implement personal boundaries while you are single, because the best breakup advice is the advice you won't need later.

Regarding sex, I will say only one thing: The longer you wait the better. Temptation and pressure to have sex will bombard you. But nothing good ever resulted from having sex too soon.

I would say that you complete me, but I'm already 100 percent totally awesome.

—Unknown

DR. TOM'S TAKE

DO YOU WANT PEACE OR POPULARITY?

As Jon's examples illustrate, everyone has experienced some level of the stress that comes with dating as a teenager. Not surprisingly, it's something that everyone can relate to. This is why we enjoy movies and books with characters that deal with these issues. Struggling to say the right thing to the person you like is a collective, shared experience. So the fact that this is happening to you doesn't make you weird. It means you're in good company with everyone else. It's helpful to start to look at ways to work with the stress of dating instead of struggling against it.

FIRST SKILL: RECOGNIZING THE BENEFITS OF STRUGGLE

Remember, it is good for your mental health to have some struggles along the way. These struggles allow you to grow and become a better version of yourself.

A good way to recognize the benefits of a struggle is to think about what happens when struggles don't occur. Think of someone you know that you would say is "spoiled." You know the type. They're bratty, self-centered, and don't appreciate the things they have. How do you think they got that way? That person is spoiled because they didn't have to struggle and work at something in the same way that you do.

Now, to be fair, we are all spoiled in some way. There are things that you take for granted that other people do not have (for example, the ability to read).

So how does this apply to the stress of dating?

First, remind yourself to have some compassion for your situation. Compassion for yourself and others is always going to help, no matter the situation. Recognize that dating and breaking up are experiences that are going to help you out in the long run. If you have to work a little bit to stay calm and not fumble over your words when you talk to someone you like, you're going to get better at it in the future because you are working on it now.

Second, when you feel like you messed up talking to someone, you make the situation worse when you tell yourself (unconsciously) it wasn't supposed to happen the way it did. This is an expectation, and having that unrealistic expectation is what makes these moments worse.

For example, Keenan is asking Leslie to the prom. But during Keenan's speech, he becomes nervous and starts talking too fast and sweating. Keenan has two ways of approaching this new development. He can either 1) accept that he is talking too fast and sweating, and just roll with it, maybe by making a joke about it, or he can 2) not accept this is happening, silently judge himself, and increase his anxiety for having a normal reaction to a stressful situation until he is in a near panic.

The goal is to recognize that we all have expectations for how we would like things to be, especially when we're talking to someone we like. However, these expectations do not always match up with the way things happen.

When you work with what is happening in the moment and let go of your expectations, your anxiety is reduced. When you hold on to the expectations and don't accept what is happening, your anxiety becomes more intense.

So how can you be more accepting, like Keenan in the first example, and let go of your expectations? Often, when teenagers (and people in general) feel like they messed up, they assume it's their fault, that it's something they should have already known or realized. You have to remind yourself that just because an interaction didn't happen the way you wanted, it doesn't mean you were wrong. It just means something different happened.

Let's start the process right now.

ACTIVITY

Challenge the Idea That You Are Wrong

On a blank sheet, draw three columns. On the first column, write what actually happened. For example, "Last Tuesday I walked by the person I like and I tripped on the carpet. I felt so stupid." On the second column, write why you think you were wrong. And then, on the final column, write the reasons why you were not totally wrong. Make sure you always have at least one more reason in the "not completely wrong column" than the "why you think you were wrong" column. For example, if you can think of four reasons why you think you were wrong, then you need to have five reasons why you were not completely wrong listed. This is to help train your brain to stop blaming yourself and be more objective with the situation.

SEX

Sex is a large part of how people measure their worth as a teenager. Getting called out as a virgin is meant to insult you as someone that's weak and immature. So, unfortunately, people will have sex with someone just to do it and get it over with. Or they have sex to let others know, in the hopes that other people will give them praise. Of course, there is the enjoyable part of sex as well, but if you feel uncomfortable about it for any reason, then the enjoyable part probably isn't the reason why you're having sex.

Simply put, if you just want to get your first time over with, are using sex to promote your social status, or are unsure for any of the million reasons that exist, hold off.

POWER OF SAYING "NO"

When talking about sex, drugs, drinking, or any other peer pressure situation, try to remember the golden rule of communication: People are allowed to ask, and you are allowed to say no, and vice versa. I will talk about why people feel the almost impossible pull to be like everyone else in the next section on popularity, but remember that you always have the option of saying no.

Saying no skillfully is the real trick because it's often taken as a reason to chide and further prod you. The important thing to remember is to not justify or explain why you are saying no. Often, other people will naturally want to attack or challenge your justifications in the hopes of getting you to say yes instead. If you don't give them a reason why you're saying no, they don't have any options. They can create all your possible motivations as they wish, but those have no weight or relevancy.

For example, if you tell your boyfriend you don't want to have sex because "If my parents found out they'd kill me," then your boyfriend can say something like, "Who cares? You didn't care what they thought last week when you went to the party."

The best option is to be a broken record and say no (without explaining why you are saying no) in a non-aggressive but affirmative way. Usually "No, I'm okay" or "No, I don't want to" work best. Changing the conversation ("Yeah, so anyways, like we were saying before ...") is sometimes necessary too.

Using the previous example, another way to say no would be for the girlfriend to tell her boyfriend, "I really care about you, but we're not having sex." And just leave it at that.

If someone keeps pressing the issue (you've had to say no more than twice) then it's okay to be more intense with your no ("I just don't want to. Stop asking.") At that point it's probably time to figure out a way to leave the situation.

Saying no skillfully takes some preparation. If you think you are going to be in a situation where you have to say no:

1. Ask yourself why you are going there in the first place.
2. Practice how you would say no using your own words so it sounds natural.

POPULARITY

Why do we feel the need to conform and be liked in the first place?

The desire to be popular (or at the very least, liked) by your peers is another common experience shared by most people. In fact, the desire to follow the leader and be part of the group is so strong that there have been a number of interesting experiments to exploit this and show how far people are willing to go. Ironically, the results were so astonishing that ethical boards and rules now prevent these types of experiments from happening.

One of the more popular experiments to show people will follow along (obey) is the Milgram experiment. At Yale University in 1963, Stanley Milgram wanted to know how far people would go, or hurt someone, when listening to and obeying the commands of a person of authority. Sounds a little like high school, right?

Stanley Milgram set up a situation where the innocent research participant thought they were electrocuting another "participant" (this person getting shocked was actually part of the research team, and not actually being hurt) because the innocent research participant was told to do so by the person running the study (the "authority" figure). The "electrical voltage" would increase as the experiment went on, with the authority figure telling the research participant to continue despite the protests of the person receiving the shock. Milgram's motivation for the study was to find out why the normally good people in Germany would support the crimes of the Nazis in World War II. He was correct in thinking and discovering that people will do hurtful things to others if they are told to do it by a person in authority. The results of the study found that 65 percent of the research participants "shocked" the other person at the highest level of 450 volts, and all the participants shocked the other person to at least 300 volts.

Another famous study looking at human behavior is the 1973 Stanford prison experiment by Philip Zimbardo. For the experiment, Zimbardo had the basement at the Stanford University psychology building converted into a mock prison. He then had student volunteers randomly divided into two groups, either as a prison guard or a prisoner. It was a very realistic role-play scenario, where the "prisoners" were arrested, fingerprinted, and "booked." Guards were given uniforms and handcuffs, and worked in typical eight-hour shifts. The plan was to observe each group's behavior over the course of two weeks, but the experiment had to be cut short after six days because of the brutal way the "guards" were treating the "prisoners." And this was only in a role-playing situation! When each student was later debriefed, most expressed shock at how they stopped acting like themselves and started acting more like a guard or prisoner. It speaks volumes about how we are influenced by our surroundings and the roles we see ourselves in.

There's also the less scary, but equally surprising, Asch conformity experiment that shows how people are likely to give the obviously wrong answer because everyone else in the group says it is right. When measuring how often people conform to the group, one-third (32 percent) of the participants went along with the group and gave a clearly wrong answer. When asked afterward why they gave an obviously wrong answer, many of them said they wanted to fit in with the group.

So, have you ever found yourself doing something to someone else (or had something done to you) because the "person in charge" made the group do it? That's what the experiments by Milgram, Zimbardo, Asch, and others are all about. But what is this desire to obey and be part of the group all about?

Well, there's a good chance our anxiety about being liked and popular can be explained by something Leon Festinger called social comparison theory in his 1954 paper on the subject. In summary, this theory says we view how we feel about ourselves based upon how we compare ourselves to other people. So, we end up constantly evaluating ourselves in different ways (intelligence, looks, money, friends, etc.) and then feel better or worse about ourselves based on this comparison.

For example, if you think that you are having a bad hair day, it influences how you feel about yourself. But why? Well, social comparison theory says that you will compare yourself to other people that are not having a bad hair day, and this comparison is what makes you feel bad. You are envious that they're not having a bad hair day like you.

On the other hand, if you do well on a test that everyone else doesn't do well on, you end up feeling better. Why is that? Well, you are comparing yourself to the performance of others, and because you did better than everyone else, you feel better about yourself. See how social comparison works?

Now, just because we naturally do this doesn't mean we are stuck doing it for life. There's a trick to catching this and not letting it ruin your day.

CHALLENGE YOUR FEELINGS OF ENVY

The very first thing to do (and the whole reason why I talked about the experiments by Milgram, Zimbardo, and Asch) is to recognize, in the moment, when these thinking errors are happening. Having the knowledge that this is happening to you at a deeper level in your thinking makes it easier to recognize when it is happening.

What you specifically want to look for in these moments is the feeling of envy. Envy is a big part of what drives our desire to be like others because we assume that if we have what they have, we will be happier. However, to be blunt, this is not true.

If you think about it, there are likely plenty of examples in your own life where you wanted something, got it, felt happier for a little bit, but then quickly went back to the way you used to feel. This can happen with things we buy, grades we receive, or goals we accomplish.

So, if we reduce our feelings of envy, we stop feeling as much anxiety about how popular we are.

How do we reduce our feelings of envy? We have to work at reducing the underlying beliefs that create the feelings of envy in the first place. We have to remind ourselves that these underlying beliefs aren't true.

For example, a guy on a basketball team could be envious that he cannot dunk like one of his teammates. What's the underlying belief? He's thinking that if he could dunk the ball, he would be seen in a more favorable way by others, and he would feel happier as a result. However, even if he learned to dunk, the positive feelings would fade over time and he would feel exactly the same as before he could dunk the ball. What he should work on is not learning how to dunk, but how he can improve as a person (better listener, better teammate, expressing empathy for others, etc.). This will allow him to be seen in a more positive way.

The goal is to ask yourself, "What is the underlying belief that is making me feel envious?" Do you think, if you had a certain body shape, people would like you more? If you were friends with that popular person, you'd feel better about yourself? Once you find out what that underlying belief is, then you can develop a plan to work on what will actually make you happier, and not work yourself up over something that isn't going to change how you feel in the long run.

Over time, recognizing these underlying beliefs is useful because they let you know that you want something, but you have to provide it for yourself. Looking externally to solve an internal issue is never going to work.

So, to sum things up, the desire to be popular and go along with what others do is an intense trait that most of us have. However, just because we feel this pull to do things that will make others like us more (even though we might not want to, like sex) doesn't mean we're stuck feeling like this. The best way to help yourself out and reduce the anxiety associated with popularity is to work with your feelings of envy.

Wish everyone at school wouldn't care so much. Dating, popularity, kids that party, etc. This is all going to be irrelevant in years and you shouldn't waste your life getting upset about temporary people. Live your life.

—Unknown

---

41. Tell that secret someone that you like them.

42. Learn to juggle.

43. Search through all the different emojis on your phone. Don't stop until you've looked at every single one. Try not to rush.

44. Put on a song, and dance. Especially if you can't dance.

45. Get social. Interestingly, socializing stimulates the production of the hormone oxytocin, creating a natural anxiety-reducing effect. Do it despite how badly you don't want to. You don't have to attend a crowded event or a party filled with lots of people you don't know. Instead, spend time with a few close friends and family members.

46. Get a foot massage, body massage, mani-pedi, or haircut. If money is tight, do an online search for a discount salon or training school that offers deeply discounted, yet quality services.

47. Phone a friend—even when you don't want to. Especially when you don't want to! Jon has avoided full-blown anxiety attacks by calling someone when all he wanted to do was isolate himself.

48. Learn a new form of exercise, such as pilates, spinning, or a kettlebell workout.

CHAPTER 7

JOBS AND MONEY

Sometimes the best part of my job is that my chair swivels.

—Office workers everywhere

WILL WORK ... IN MODERATION

Growing up, I had to suck on Motrin pills to appease my sweet tooth, as sugar and candy were forbidden in our home. I often failed to spit them out in time, but the analgesic aftertaste was worth the brief reward. When I was able to obtain sugary sweets, it was most often PEZ. I wouldn't care if I ate them from a pink Hello Kitty dispenser. I still receive PEZ candy dispensers on holidays, and I savor each confectionery tablet. I typically dump the dispensers and mainline the candy from the wrapped packs. As a kid, I would scarf the pieces in seconds, which produced soaring blood-glucose levels. The sugar high would result in a temporary Scarface persona. In lieu of a machine gun strapped to each arm and cocaine residue splattered across my face, I hauled ass down the sidewalk on my Big Wheel with a squirt gun in my right hand and orange, PEZ-tinged lips.

As with many maladaptive behaviors, I can blame my parents. Banishing sugar from the diets of my brother, Jeff, and me could only backfire. Despite their good intentions, years of parent-imposed sugar abstinence caused us to crave candy like street junkies with the shakes and no means of procuring it. The only reason I wanted to grow up was to get money and hoard barrels of candy.

As Dr. McDonagh summarizes later in this chapter, teens want to work in order to buy stuff. Once Jeff and I reached a semi-employable age (12 or so), Jeff was able to procure sugary rations through periodic employment. He mowed lawns, painted fences, and delivered newspapers around the neighborhood. Already privy to the miseries of the burgeoning working class, I stalled entry into the child workforce and relied solely upon cunning and thievery to get candy. But I lacked the prowess of an experienced juvenile delinquent, and I was caught more often than not.

On numerous occasions, mom dragged me by the ear back to the store—my tongue blue, and pockets bulging with sweet loot—where she forced me to confess my sins to the store manager, and hand over money for what I had eaten. It was demoralizing, but not enough to end my budding criminal enterprise. I never stole anything of actual street value. Instead, I acquired small items that were high in corn syrup.

> *Math Problem: Jon has 33 candy bars. He eats 29. What does he have now? Diabetes.*

But I soon hit pay dirt. This Shangri-La of sugar took the form of my brother's hidden stash in his dresser drawer. To the adolescent, Jeff's top dresser drawer was the equivalent of the entire bottom shelf of the candy aisle at 7-Eleven. He had everything a rotten-tooth consumer could want. The actual volume of candy that had secretly made it into our home was surreal. Jeff would surely do hard time if caught, and my brother was anything but clandestine. Fortunately for me, he was also a bigger deviant. I carefully observed his day-to-day activities and quickly recognized a pattern of malfeasance. Every day that kid was breaking a litany of rules and regulations set forth by my father. Soon, the blackmail ensued. I learned that I could threaten Jeff with snitching to Mom and Dad about any one of his shady antics, and he would painfully relinquish a 1-pound bag of plain or peanut M&M's. And it didn't stop there. It wasn't long before I owned most of his durable goods through simple extortion. I was the new owner of a Sony Walkman, a Spalding catcher's mitt, an aluminum Easton baseball bat, a Pioneer stereo, and multiple CD box sets. This entire inventory was scuttled from his room to mine under a cloak of obscurity. Despite his sleeping naked on a yoga mat with only a candle for light, my parents proudly assumed he had become a minimalist. It's almost sad how oblivious they were to what they misread as a philanthropic transfer of goods from one misguided sibling to another.

But like any oppressed being, Jeff's spirit animal eventually took over. He told my parents everything, and my sugar train ended. I was grounded for weeks, forced to eat nutrient-dense complex carbs, and sentenced to months of employment shredding pillars of stacked paper tax documents in the storage closet of my mom's accounting office. I was a modern-day chain gang of one.

Like Jeff, most teens work because they're motivated by the desire to buy things. Teens typically spend their money on car expenses, personal recreation, clothing, educational expenses like saving for college, and helping their families with cost-of-living expenses (e.g., rent, groceries). I ultimately worked because it's what we all did growing up middle class in the suburbs. It's how we bought kites, Star Wars figures, BMX parts to upgrade our motocross bikes, movies, CDs, and eventually, gas for muscle cars that got 9 mpg downhill. My aversion to continuous work in my teens meant that I rarely had money for anything. I wasn't actually lazy; I simply lacked a calling.

I don't think necessity is the mother of invention. Invention, in my opinion, arises directly from idleness, possibly also from laziness—to save oneself trouble.

—Agatha Christie

SOCIOECONOMIC STATUS

Both of my parents worked long hours, sacrificing vacations, cable TV, and real cheese to put Jeff and me through private school. We attended a small charter school with a cross section of spoiled kids that were in a caste foreign to our own. They had no concept of powdered milk, hand-me-down clothing, or home haircuts. This was most evident in the student parking lot where new and custom cars lined painted stalls.

The worst of the worst at my school was Michelle Moneypants, who received a baby blue Mercedes convertible for her 15th birthday. Her family lived atop the tallest peak above our town, complete with a helipad for her self-important father. I never saw Michelle or her younger sister (Mini Moneypants) in the same designer clothes twice. I'm certain their attire was discarded after use while a couturier tailored new clothes in their covert textile mill. Special-event clothing was purveyed directly from merchants in Milan, of course. The Moneypants sisters exuded wealth and privilege.

They were rich, talented, and beautiful. So it was easy to hate them for their credit lines and radiant skin. Their house still stands above my hometown today, snubbing the middle- and working-class residents below. I silently wished for a meteor to strike the Moneypants estate. It never happened, but only because they also owned outer space. The Moneypants kids and many like them at my school had no concept of work, except what they observed at home by landscapers and chambermaids. They were especially confused by my brother and me walking miles to and from school. This single act relegated our socioeconomic status to "unfortunate."

In the movie Becoming Jane, Reverend Austen said it best when he stated, "Nothing destroys spirit like poverty." Research indicates that socioeconomic status (SES) is a key factor that influences quality of life for children, youth, and families. SES affects human functioning in many ways, including development across the lifespan, psychological health, and physical health. Increasing evidence supports the link between lower SES and negative psychological health outcomes, while more positive psychological outcomes such as optimism, self-esteem, and perceived control have been linked to higher levels of SES for youth. Lower levels of SES have been found to be associated with higher levels of emotional and behavioral difficulties, including anxiety, depression, attention deficit/hyperactivity disorder, and conduct disorders.

PROS AND CONS OF TEEN EMPLOYMENT

When I yielded to consistent employment, my first real job was delivering a free weekly newspaper called the *Dollar Saver*. Due to a blend of teen lethargy and anxiety-related paranoia regarding snipers along my route, I rolled all the papers at home so my parents could see and then pitched them into a nearby dumpster each week, after which I'd sit in the park conspiring shortcuts around hard work. It took a few months, but I was finally fired due to complaints from residents not receiving their paper on the porch, which makes sense because they were miles away in a dumpster. My next esteemed role was as cashier at Burger King. But I was demoted after falling victim to a female short-change artist, and had to work the fryer, where I was prone to regular skin break-outs from being sheened in vat grease. From there, I graduated to the tuber business in the mall food court at an eatery called Tater Junction, where, despite reeking of butter-soaked chives, I had my choice of dates throughout the food court. I couldn't land a girl from Bloomingdale's or Forever 21, but I had my pick among the ranks at Sbarro, Cinnabon, and Orange Julius. I settled in with Valerie from Donut World. We dated for months until I tired of apple fritters and she of tater tots.

Along the way, I also had short labor stints doing yard work for a lady with a hole in her throat that she talked through like a cancer kazoo; at a clandestine industrial building that raised rats for research (I quit after the first day, took one of the rats with me, and named him "Snowball"); as a city government errand boy; at ACE Hardware; arranging fake potted plants at a silk flower store; emptying parking meters at my college campus police department; and my single favorite job, at a tanning salon disinfecting the sweat puddles of the prettiest, most toasted girls I knew.

Though I didn't realize it, even during inconsistent employment, I was gaining transferable life skills beyond baking tubers or tanorexics.

Teenagers who work in high school end up with better adult jobs and higher incomes, according to studies, as well as stronger "soft skills" like dependability, punctuality, confidence, and communication.

BENEFITS TO TEEN EMPLOYMENT
- Acquiring valuable work experience
- Learning to effectively budget for expenses and manage finances

- Accumulating professional references and networking opportunities
- Gaining a constructive use of free time while losing time to engage in risky behaviors
- Learning and sharpening time-management skills
- Developing good work habits
- Gaining marketable skills such as improving interpersonal and business communication, learning conflict resolution, handling money, and developing interview skills for future professional roles
- Gaining newfound confidence, increased responsibility, and independence

NEGATIVE CONSEQUENCES OF TEEN EMPLOYMENT

- Less time for homework. Working students may not have or make enough time to complete their work.
- Higher rates of absenteeism and less school involvement. A job reduces available study and sleep time. Fatigue or lack of prep for the day's academic tasks may lead to skipping school, and a job may replace extracurricular activities.
- Lower grades. Students who work more than 20 hours a week have overall lower GPAs than their peers who work 10 or fewer hours a week.
- More likely to use drugs and alcohol. Research suggests that substance abuse is higher for students who work 20 or more hours per week.
- Bad perception of work itself. Depending on the type of job, early entry into a negative or harsh work environment may encourage negative views of work.
- Increased stress from trying to balance work and school.

Money often costs too much.

—Ralph Waldo Emerson

So, what do Dr. McDonagh and I suggest to you regarding work?

Paid work has core value far beyond a paycheck, and teens (including those who plan to attend college) who don't work may hinder themselves. Choosing not to work a paid job has drawbacks. "There's some other research that suggests, especially for teens that aren't bound for college, if they don't work in high school, they have worse employment outcomes," says Martha Ross, a fellow at the Metropolitan Policy Program at the Brookings Institution. "It bodes ill for them down the line that they're missing an important on-ramp into the working world." The ideal teen work scenario seems to be a job that requires few hours per week during the school year.

Research has shown that college completion rates are highest among those who worked 15 hours a week or less when they were high school seniors.

Try to keep the number of hours at 15 or fewer per week during the school year. Research suggests that students that work 10 hours or less a week gain the benefits of employment, while students that work over 20 hours a week suffer the negative consequences of work mentioned earlier. Keep school as your top priority. You can always make money, but you can never make or buy more time.

Interestingly, fewer teens are in the marketplace today versus previous decades, and the downside is that many employers complain that these teens lack simple soft skills like getting to work on time, dealing effectively with a manager, teamwork, or exhibiting a positive attitude. Young adults are entering the labor force with less job experience than earlier generations. Entry-level jobs teach you humility, maturity, and the basic employment skills that we need to become nice humans.

Today's teens may not be working in greater numbers, but they're certainly not turning into hammock sloths. Many teens today are fully immersed in equally beneficial activities as employment. A high percentage is in summer school, while others are volunteering, studying abroad, fulfilling internships, or participating in other commendable endeavors to remain marketable and competitive. For the anxious teen, a job has the dual benefit of both providing needed structure and preparing for an industrious and rewarding future.

A job teaches youth the importance of showing up on time, keeping to a schedule, completing tasks, and being accountable to an objective third party who might coach via constructive criticism and negative feedback that teens have yet to receive elsewhere. It's a necessary dose of reality not always dispensed at home. Working part time while going to school requires some self-awareness beyond a willingness to work hard to get the job done. Texting friends, checking social media, arriving late and/or leaving early are poor working behaviors that will reflect negatively on you. If you're going to do a job, whether it's yard work, dog walking, or restaurant or retail work, take pride in your contributions. No matter how small you consider your efforts, they make a difference. At the very least, you are being aptly honed into greatness.

But don't cut corners just because of your lesser-known anxiety superpower. You may likely have a competitive edge in balancing work and school like a boss. Results of a Canadian study found that people who spend a lot of time thinking about a problem tend to have higher verbal intelligence. The research indicated three possible explanations for the association—psychological, neurological, and evolutionary: "The psychological hypothesis proposes that since people who are stressed spend more time rethinking and analyzing about different issues, they perhaps understand about events and ideas better than others. The neurological hypothesis says people who stress more have a higher amount of white matter. Since white matter is primarily the neuronal connections that act as a conduit between different regions of the brain, a larger proportion of it facilitates faster communication between the various brain regions and results in more swift responses. The evolutionary hypothesis, on the other hand, suggests ruminators have a survival benefit as their tendency to preplan things prepares them for eventualities."

With great power comes great responsibility.

—Spiderman

 DR. TOM'S TAKE

WORK, BECAUSE NOTHING'S FOR FREE

The pressure to be a student and have a part-time job can be overwhelming at times. Balancing priorities at school and having a job require careful planning and good time management skills. If you don't have a plan in place and misuse your free time, it's practically a given that moments of anxiety like those Jon described are going to happen.

While not everyone has a job, it's likely that you're involved in something else outside of the classroom that takes up time. If you don't have a job, think about that other activity as though it is your job—whether it's sports, an after-school club, family responsibilities, volunteer work, tutoring, etc. These are the things that are important in your life, but take away from your study time.

Prior to applying for part-time work, there are two things to consider:

First, it's important to remind yourself that a job is not your first priority as a teenager. School ranks above a job. You want to be the boss in the future, right? So, it's important you look for a job that supports your endeavors and fits with your schedule.

If possible, avoid a situation where you feel your boss is placing too much pressure on you. A good way to measure the impact of a job on your life is if the important things start to suffer. Your grades, overall mental health in the form of stress and anxiety, and how you're getting along with other people are good points to measure. If you find that you're stuck working late hours on weekdays or your boss is making unreasonable demands on your time, then it's probably time you switched jobs. A part-time job is a means to an end. You're not getting paid to go to school, but school will pay the bigger dividends later.

Second, you are allowed to ask for your scheduling needs to be met in the interview process. Before you accept any job, make sure you and your future boss understand and agree on what is expected before you start. For example, if you can only work on Friday evenings and

Saturdays, be sure to let them know this up front. Understandably, this can be a scary prospect, especially if you really want the job or this is your first time interviewing. During any job interview, it's common to want to sell yourself to the manager so you'll be hired. As a result, sometimes teenagers feel they are not allowed to mention things (like time restrictions) that might prevent them from getting the job. However, the interview is the best time to ask for the schedule and hours you think you would work.

Remember, during the interview, it's not just them evaluating you, it's you evaluating them. You get to interview them as well. You are a valued asset. If you don't like the answers to questions asked of them, you don't have to take the job. In fact, if there are red flags or you don't feel like they would be able to support your schedule, then a polite "No, thank you" from your side is the best response. There is power in saying no.

So, let's say you've gone through the interview process and you're working at a place that understands your time constraints, but you're still feeling overwhelmed. Here's how you can approach it.

ACTIVITY
Time Management Skill

The goal of this skill is to train yourself to prioritize your day's activities. You can plan for some things, but not others. No matter the circumstance, learning how to break things up in these four categories will always help you manage your time.

Divide a sheet of paper into four sections as follows:

1. Urgent Important
2. Not Urgent Important
3. Urgent Not Important
4. Not Urgent Not Important

Urgent and Important: These are the things that would be considered a real emergency, triggering the fight-or-flight response.

Examples for this category include medical emergencies, life-threatening situations, or very important projects that have long-term impact.

It's important to remember that most things do not fall under this category, even though you might feel like it's an emergency in the moment. You weren't designed to be in fight-or-flight mode all the time and do not want to spend most of your time here.

Not Urgent, but Important: Think of this time slot as the place you want to be most of the time. That's because this time is for the things in life that will be important, but don't need to happen right now. If you don't use this time slot well, then all the important things suddenly become last minute, and that's what places you in fight-or-flight mode. Think of Not Urgent, but Important as the planning stage. For example, if you have a paper that is due in a week, this is the time to start writing a few paragraphs. You can also think about using this time to do things for yourself or others that you enjoy. This includes eating right, exercising, and attending to the important relationships in your life.

Urgent, but Not Important: Recognizing when you're in this time slot is important because this is the section where you can likely make the most improvements. Most people tend to waste their time with things they think are urgent, but in the big picture, are not important. For example, texting a friend back when you're supposed to be studying. We think that it's urgent for us to get back to our friends right away (making us feel like it's urgent) when really it's more important that you use that time to finish studying. Cell phone use in general falls into this category. If you let yourself finish the task at hand, you can then send a quick text to catch up.

Not Urgent and Not Important: This time slot is essentially for those things that you probably like to do, but spend too much time with, and they become time wasters. Playing cell phone games, streaming videos, watching TV, getting lost on TikTok. These are activities that are fine for a few minutes, but can become an issue if they take up too much time. Spending too much time in this space makes you look irresponsible to others and creates all the other problems that go along with that image.

Now, fill in each section according to your average day. Include all job and non-job activities. You then have two goals:

1. Look at all the things classified as urgent (in sections 1 and 3) and work on moving them into the Not Urgent, but Important section. You want to keep this area free for real emergencies. The goal is to see that not

everything is a life-threatening emergency, even though it might feel that way. To do this, ask yourself what you can do that will make this less urgent. It might involve keeping your Google Calendar more up to date, finishing a paper early, or saying "no" to people if you feel like you have too many commitments.

2. Look at all those fun activities in the Not Urgent and Not Important box, and stop doing them on such a regular basis. These activities are time sponges, and they create panic and urgency. In small doses, they're great, but too much of them is definitely a problem.

It might be helpful to fill out this chart daily for several weeks. The repetition will help you start to recognize that there is a way to make things less urgent and to limit the amount of time you spend on Not Urgent and Not Important activities.

THE PRESSURES OF MONEY

Jobs provide you with an education outside of the classroom, provide real work experience, and teach you time management and the value of a dollar. But we all know the real reason for getting a job: money! You want to get paid so you can buy stuff. And there's nothing wrong with that. Being able to buy something is a great feeling. It provides you with a sense of independence and teaches you that you can do things for yourself. It's a great self-esteem booster.

But sometimes there are pressures associated with buying things, and that can be problematic.

Do you feel like you have to own what everyone else has? Maybe you think other people won't like you if you don't have the newest "thing."

Or, worse, people will be nice to your face, but then say things behind your back? "Didn't she wear that shirt last week?" Maybe you are used to people complimenting you on the things you own, and you think without them, your friends won't like you as much. Or, perhaps, taking the bus to school instead of driving your own car is considered social suicide. There are many reasons why people feel the need to keep up appearances. The concern about what your friends think of you is called peer pressure. Wanting the money to buy things that are influenced by what other people think can be difficult.

So, how do you deal with the subtle and sometimes not so subtle peer pressure to have things?

The most effective approach is to look at your friend group. If you feel like your friends are the type to make fun of anyone who doesn't have the "right thing" (clothes, car, phone, headphones, etc.), then you need to ask yourself, "Why am I hanging out with these people?"

ACTIVITY

The List of Five

Take a blank sheet of paper or open a Word document and draw a line down the middle.

On the left side, write down the top five qualities you would like to have in any friend (not in a particular friend, but in general). What are the top five qualities that you think make someone a good friend? While this can be anything, from the types of music they enjoy to the type of family they come from, try to include the big-picture stuff too, such as being a good person, comfortable to be around, being trustworthy, and being a good listener. If you come up with more than five qualities, that's great! But do your best to narrow it down to the five that have the highest priority to you.

On the right side of the paper, write down the top five qualities of the friend (or acquaintance) that is making you feel peer pressure. Again, if you can come up with more than five, that's great, but make sure to keep the five that are most important to you.

If you can, do The List of Five before reading on. Sometimes it's better to do an exercise before you know what the exercise is looking for.

What we're hoping for is that most, if not all, of your top five qualities on the right side match up with the qualities on the left side. When you are friends with people that match up with the list on the left, you'll always feel better. These are the people that are going to help you feel good about yourself.

There's also a good chance that because you trust them, you can accept authentic advice that won't make you feel upset at the end of the day. Sometimes helpful words hurt to hear at first. "Hey, your face is breaking out. I have some acne cream you can try." People sometimes argue, and that is okay and normal. The important thing is that you feel supported by this person at the end of day.

Note: When asking yourself, "Why am I hanging out with this person?" The hope is that you can come up with a reason other than "I want to be/stay popular." Friends that we have only because we want to climb the social ladder make us feel anxious and don't bring out our best qualities.

Remember, having a job and balancing your time with the social pressures of being a teenager is a normal experience. Feeling stressed about these issues is expected. If you follow the skills above, you will gradually feel more competent and bring your anxiety down to manageable levels.

The grand essentials of happiness are: something to do, something to love, and something to hope for.

—George Washington Burnap, author of *The Sphere and Duties of Woman: A Course of Lectures*

WAYS TO ALLEVIATE ANXIETY

49. Begin learning a new language.

50. Volunteer. Helping others has the dual benefit of (1) Getting you out of your head and off your own problems; and (2) Helping others and feeling good about it in return. Find opportunities here: www.volunteer.gov and www.volunteermatch.org.

51. Find a hill and run up, then walk down, repeating this until you are tired. It's okay if it only takes one time.

52. Walk into a room; in one minute, try to memorize exactly how it looks. When the minute is up, walk into a different room and draw or write down the image you have in your mind.

53. Make a paper airplane travel as far as possible.

54. Learn how to flip a pen around your thumb.

55. Try to memorize 20 anxiety-reducing tactics from this book.

56. Memorize a few lines or a paragraph of a famous speech or monologue (e.g. the Gettysburg Address, Martin Luther King Jr.'s "I Have a Dream" speech, or the opening to *Richard III*).

CHAPTER 8

ANXIETY RELATED TO THE FUTURE

The greatest weapon against stress is our ability to choose one thought over another.

—William James

THE SKY IS FALLING ... OR, IS IT?

The emotional content of films and television programs can affect your psychological health. It can do this by directly affecting your mood, and your mood can then affect many aspects of your thinking and behavior. But there is also an increasing tendency for news broadcasters to "emotionalize" their news and to do so by emphasizing any potential negative outcomes of a story no matter how low the risks of those negative outcomes might be. Exaggerating or otherwise distorting the news to give it more emotional flare is part of TV journalists' fight to remain relevant and competitive. With so many journalists covering the same topics, someone is going to up the impact ante by whatever means necessary. This is basically scaremongering at every available opportunity in order to sensationalize the impact of a news story.

Is there a psychological impact of exposure to tragedy at a distance?

This feeds right into man's natural evolutionary trait to affix more to the bad than the good. It's how we quickly identified threats in our primitive days. But this can result in symptoms similar to post-traumatic stress disorder (PTSD). Overindulging in bad news isn't a survival technique today—it only creates more anxiety. (Later in this chapter, Dr. McDonagh will walk you through specific skills to counteract this negativity overload.)

A 1997 study looked at the psychological effects of viewing negative news items. Three different 14-minute news bulletins were constructed. One was made entirely of negative news items, one was made of entirely positive news items (e.g., people winning the lottery, recovering from illness, etc.), and one was made up of items that were emotionally neutral. The bulletins were shown to three different groups of people. As predicted, those who watched the negative news bulletin all reported being significantly more anxious and sadder after watching this bulletin than those people who watched either the positive or neutral news bulletin. The people who had watched the negative news bulletin spent more time thinking and talking about their worry and were more likely to catastrophize it than people in the other two groups. So, not only are negative news broadcasts likely to make you sadder and more anxious, they are also likely to exacerbate your own personal worries and anxieties. It can potentially exacerbate a range of personal concerns not specifically relevant to the content of the program itself.

Mary McNaughton-Cassill, a professor at the University of Texas, San Antonio, and leading researcher on the connection between media consumption and stress, conducted research that suggests, "In addition to a burgeoning sense of helplessness, cognitive shortcuts triggered by the news can also lead us to gradually see the world as a darker and darker place, chipping away at certain optimistic tendencies."

Like vaping, self-tattooing, and licking escalator rails, exposure to negative news is literally bad for your health. Media outlets don't get paid to deliver good news because it doesn't sell. We live in a culture of alarmism where the glut of bad news yields fear, aggression, and anxiety. And it's a one-two punch because it does this while blocking your happiness, peace of mind, and creative thinking.

It's not that the world has actually gotten worse, but a prolific media is relentlessly reporting it in HD pessimism. The only winners in this unhealthy arrangement are the advertisers who regularly interrupt the 24-hour live stream of wheelchair thieves and otter-punchers to scare us into buying more life insurance and antianxiety pills. Bad news is toxic and jacks up your perception of what you should be paying attention to. Things you need to think about, like studying for midterms or getting enough sleep, are overlooked, while the stuff that shouldn't be troubling you, like maniacal overseas dictators, override your mind. Issues like radicalism get hyped while the effects of chronic anxiety on your body are ignored entirely. That's healthy perspective turned on its head. Bad news affects us physiologically. Bad news triggers the brain's limbic system, spurring a release of cortisol, a stress hormone that deregulates the immune system and inhibits the release of growth hormones. It'll turn you into a tiny madman running amok in a prolonged temper tantrum. This is likely how you feel after a sizeable dose of bad news—small, angry, and anxious.

The nightly news is nightly negativity. But unless you catch a long flight to Mars, it's tough to dodge the daily torrent of anxiety-stimulating news. Sometimes it feels like things are getting worse, as if society is climbing toward the "dreadfully appalling" threshold. Bad news can quickly spur anxiety and depression. Look no further than the CNN ticker tape at the bottom of your TV screen to shotgun negativity into your psyche and create palpable anxiety.

The upside is that there's one simple cure: Limit your consumption. We can't control the turmoil around us. But we can dramatically limit our exposure, counter the negative with positive, and recognize that cheesy, gelled, and lacquered TV journalists exist only to have you suckle at the bad news teat. The more visceral and gnarly the news reported, the more eyes are watching. But you don't need to be inundated to be informed.

A day of worry is more exhausting than a week of work.
—John Lubbock

To be clear, neither Dr. McDonagh nor I suggest that you bury your head in a hole and remain ignorant; rather, limit your exposure to the nightly negative deluge, and/or consider other sources of information, like NPR and the Discovery Channel. Temper your negative news exposure with regular doses of humor, good news, and Animal Planet.

In case you don't, there are antidotes to the negative effects of watching bad news in the form of relaxation, exercise, or distraction, such as reading this informative book. Consider the findings of a 2007 study by the *International Journal of Behavioral Medicine*:

> The psychological effects of televised news were studied in 2 groups (n = 179) of undergraduate students who watched a 15-minute random newscast followed by either a 15-minute progressive

relaxation exercise or a 15-minute lecture (control condition). Subjective measures of state anxiety, total mood disturbance (TMD), positive affect, and negative affect were obtained before and after the news, as well as following relaxation exercise or the lecture. The results show that state anxiety and TMD increased, whereas positive affect decreased in both groups after watching the news, and 15 minutes later, they returned to baseline (pre-news) only in the relaxation group, whereas they remained unchanged in the control group. These findings demonstrate that watching the news on television triggers persisting negative psychological feelings that could not be buffered by attention-diverting distraction (i.e., lecture), but only by a directed psychological intervention such as progressive relaxation.

TODAY'S ANXIETY THREAT: "HIGH"

Here's more good news! The mainstream media does not paint an accurate picture of reality. The world is vast and rife with tons of positive things continually taking place. But it feels the opposite because our brains cling to the bad.

Consider the single-cell invader—the *Naegleria fowleri* (aka brain-eating amoeba). It's a parasite that loves yummy bacteria, but will settle for your tasty brain if it veers off course. According to the Centers for Disease Control and Prevention (CDC), brains are accidental food for *N. fowleri* when the amoeba gets into a human through the nose. Infection occurs unknowingly from diving, wakeboarding, or performing water sports, when water is forced into the nose. Infections have even occurred in people who dipped their heads into hot springs or flushed their sinuses with tap water. Wait … what?! There was the alarm for me, an anxious daily nasal rinse user: Someone actually died from a nasal rinse. Which is why I started freaking out and boiling bottled water. That poor guy might've saved my life. Probably not.

While the single-cell invader is a tragic major news story whenever a hapless victim snorts the wrong water and dies, it is not a valid risk with which I should have been concerned. Not even close. But that didn't stop me from paying mental homage to the sinister amoeba during my daily nasal rinses. Until the carnivorous amoeba made headlines, I was using untreated tap water for years to blast 16 ounces of possibly parasite-ridden municipal water through my sinuses. Nothing ate my brain. Or it might have, and I didn't notice. Maybe I was on the cusp of a career in rocket science, but ended up a writer because I have a half-eaten brain. Had I known that out of the millions of recreational water exposures that occur each year, only 0 to 8 *Naegleria fowleri* infections are identified, it would not have made my Credible Threat Matrix at all.

Today, social media is in cahoots with the news. Consider the 2015 study in *Cyberpsychology, Behavior, and Social Networking*, in which 753 middle school and high school students were surveyed. Researchers found that those who spent more than two hours a day on social networking sites like Instagram or TikTok were more likely to report distress, poor mental health, and even suicidal thoughts. However, the relationship between the use of these Web-based platforms and mental health problems in children and adolescents is unclear.

Keeping a constant presence online causes you to lose sleep and feel anxious and depressed. Long ago, I made a rule to only read or watch news related to pet adoption rallies or criminals who fortuitously shot themselves in the face. I also replaced all news-related apps with interesting or satirical news from *The Onion, Discovery News, The Chive, Cracked, Upworthy,* etc., I run regular purges on social media deleting any users, pages, organizations, etc., that push negativity my way. This was initially tough because I'm on the California coastline, where earthquakes are common. My primary fear in media-detoxing was that a quake would occur—especially a deep one under the Pacific Ocean we'd never feel—and I wouldn't know that a tsunami was coming. I soon realized that I could just watch for thousands of people running to higher ground and then follow.

Happiness is not something ready-made. It comes from your own actions.

—Dalai Lama

ANXIETY CAN THRIVE ANYWHERE

Overall I would define my era of upbringing as not particularly stress-heavy. We had the Cold War, side ponytails, and Day-Glo clothing. The music consisted of effeminate hairbands whose members wore Spandex and profound layers of eye shadow. Lashing out didn't mean shooting someone in the face; it meant getting a weird haircut, then dying it blue and green. We made mixtapes and wondered if Russian subs filled with starving communists would indiscriminately fire nuclear missiles at the West Coast. Free time was spent outdoors in trees, under cars, on rooftops, and in dirt-floor makeshift forts.

We were free-range humans, and child abduction rarely crossed our minds because we had pocket knives and lean muscle mass if someone tried. No one wore sunblock. A healthy breakfast had the word "sugar" in the name, and making book covers for our textbooks from paper grocery bags was mandatory every fall. We stayed outside until the streetlights came on, soaring unencumbered from 2-foot bike ramps because we weren't wrapped in helmets and padding. It was a carefree era when kids weren't coddled.

Yet I didn't feel carefree at all. Anxiety took that away from me. Even though the world felt simpler in my teens, anxiety can thrive anywhere and works with what's available. I had some of my worst anxiety while at an all-inclusive resort in the Caribbean. I ended up cutting the trip short and flying home three days early because of it. Anxiety hates to relax; but that doesn't mean you can't. Recall that anxiety involves exaggerated worries and expectations of negative outcomes in unknown situations. It's worry, fear, and dread that are not commensurate with the actual situation. Even in the absence of external negative stimulus, an anxious mind will often create some from scratch. Your physical setting aside, anxiety is far more about your state of mind and where your thoughts are than where you are physically. In other words, you can be smack in the middle of a chaotic, crowded concert and feel more relaxed than while sitting at your hotel concierge desk trying to choose between Snuba and spearfishing.

BEWARE OF WHAT-IFS

Many of us place too much weight on what-ifs. This is troubling in that it fuels anxiety. What-ifs are the incendiary tinder tossed into the anxiety kiln. But by controlling the what-ifs, you will dramatically reduce your anxiety. What-ifs sap power by projecting your focus into the unknown future. Keep your power rooted in the now. The future comes one moment at a time, and you can only live in that moment. Why do you want to trip forward? It's not only impossible, it's futile. Instead, flip the script. Change the what-ifs into positives: "What if I kick ass?" "What if the teacher uses my grade to set the curve?" "What if I convert my greatest fears into my greatest successes?" How many times have your worst-case fear scenarios been wrong? I'm guessing nearly every time. I can honestly not recall a personal worst-case fear ever turning into reality for me. Not once. But I can recount 100 times that things turned 180-degrees better than I'd what-iffed.

You feel the way you do right now because of the thoughts you are thinking at this moment.
—David D. Burns, author of *Feeling Good: The New Mood Therapy*

NEW MOOD THERAPY

When I left the stability of a corporate career to start writing full time, I what-iffed all over myself. "What if I'm never published? What if nobody buys my books? What if I have to move back into my childhood bedroom with my two cats?" The only thing I've had any control over is my effort within any given moment, and the fact that I will never read a review—good or bad.

I eased the what-ifs by embedding myself in the moment as I wrote, and I remained in each moment as it came. I focused only on what I was creating in any given second, sentence by sentence. I gave each word and sentence the power and attention it deserved without the distraction of what-ifs. I worked this way until I had completed the following:

- Written my first book proposal.
- Collaborated with a clinical cowriter and illustrator.
- Obtained a literary agent.
- Hired an attorney.
- Created a manuscript.
- Received some publishing offers.
- Signed my first contract.

I never paused to what-if again; I just kept writing. I didn't even stop to celebrate my achievements. I wanted to; I just couldn't afford it. I had to keep working, or move into my car. Even now I work to stay rooted in each moment. Don't worry; it becomes much easier with practice. Consider a world-class athlete who is honed into one skill and one practice session at a time until he or she becomes one of the best. By focusing your energy on the present moment, each moment becomes the most intense and refined, making the end product the best book, athlete, painting, SAT score, or <insert your own accomplishment> ever.

Life is what happened when all the what-ifs didn't.

—Jodi Picoult, author

CATASTROPHIZING

DANGER: If you don't moderate the what-ifs early on, you risk a painful side effect called catastrophizing. It's a cognitive distortion where the mind convinces you of something that isn't true. We'll also call it "future-tripping." Soon, fear and anxiety may become your nagging life partner, convincing you that everything is worse than it actually is. This is how I catastrophized myself into that sad cubicle job after grad school. I let the what-ifs take hold until I chose the path of least resistance and a steady paycheck. Yet each morning my intuition cried,

"You're a sell-out! And why are you wearing pleated khakis?!" I would stuff the voice back down with more stock options and free breakroom snacks. I had let anxiety take the wheel, determining every decision from what I ordered at the company cafeteria to what I'd hang on beige cubicle walls.

What started out as letting my anxiety control small decisions turned into anxiety-gone-wild that determined everything I did. Anxiety and catastrophizing adversely impact your well-being in that they trigger your stress-response system and put you in a needlessly amplified state of awareness. This exacerbates the situation as it undermines your ability to create a more positive and realistic outcome. You don't need to be in this heightened mental state; you're not fighting a T. Rex. Don't let the world creep in and harsh your mellow. Learn more strategies to avoid catastrophizing from Dr. McDonagh.

CALMING TECHNIQUES

Telling someone who's anxious to "get over it" is like telling a blind person to "just look harder." It's not as easy as an "on/off" switch.

If you ever have an anxiety attack in front of others, you're likely to receive the universal response, "Calm down." Unless you have mastered the art of instant self-soothing, it's unlikely you can make yourself calm down on command. Recall that anxiety disorders cause your body to enter a fight-or-flight state in conditions where it's needless, like when you get cut off on the freeway, and then honk at the hapless driver, who responds with the middle finger and brake-checking you. You would likely incur a few moments of unrequited rage toward the person, but social customs and the law require that no matter the rudeness of others, we are not to stalk them off the interstate to exact revenge with a tire iron. Instead, you're left with a racing heart, fast breathing, and tension throughout your body that you don't need. This is how I would often find myself in daily life—in an intense state of hypervigilance, perpetually amped, and ready for chaos that never came. It might make sense if I were a marine deployed to the Middle East rather than a writer in a swanky, urban cafe where my biggest threat was being served decaf.

You can't instantly calm down, but you can use simple techniques to get there, starting with a predetermined plan to deal with anxiety as it arises. In other words, "Assemble your troops before you need them!" One of my simplest tactics is to quickly move away from the source of stress. In the aforementioned road rage scenario, I'd take the next available exit to peace-out for a while. If it's a difficult person I have to see regularly at school or work, it's not as easy. A problem with anxiety disorders is that you can't always physically leave the scene to move from anxious to calm. And you can't stuff them into the janitorial closet (legally). This is where the soothing skills below will help you.

- Physically move away from the source of anxiety when possible.
- Shun negativity in all forms.
- Stay in the present moment.
- Kick ass.

Relaxation likely feels foreign to you. I sometimes get anxious if I'm not feeling anxious; as if there's something I should be worried about, but forgot. I will misinterpret the stillness as "the calm before the storm," rather than what it is: peace that I rightfully deserve. This is why consistently practicing relaxation techniques is so imperative, so that regardless of your anxiety levels, you can get yourself back to baseline quickly, without feeling so strange to experience internal peace.

> *I think I'm afraid to be happy because whenever I get too happy, something bad always happens.*
>
> —Charlie Brown

Besides the 101 tactics we share throughout this text, there are some examples:

- Color in a teen/adult coloring book (I'm hooked on this).
- Partake in guided relaxation/meditations (search for the free ones in your apps store).
- Look at the "anxiety" or "relaxation" board on Pinterest.

 DR. TOM'S TAKE

BRINGING YOUR ATTENTION TO THE PRESENT MOMENT

The increase in technology and social media has given today's teenagers earlier exposure to the dangers of the world. And, as Jon described, this exposure can create anxiety for some teens. It's an unfortunate side effect of our developing world. Granted, it's better than generations before having to go to work at six years old on the family farm or in the factory to help provide for your family. But in the past few years, the state of the world, in both its positive and negative splendor, is broadcast into short, attention-grabbing sound bites and images

The reason it isn't fair is because too much awareness at an inappropriate age can create anxiety. Couple this fact with our focus on terrorism, school shootings, and pandemics, and it's easy to see why the early exposure to the world's issues can feel inappropriate for the age.

When we are young we seek out safety and security. In order to develop "healthy" attachments to others and have a positive view of the world and our future, it's necessary for us to know that we are safe. For some of us, for our own valid reasons, things that challenge this idea of a safe world—like early exposure to war conflicts—can contribute to anxiety.

There were certainly threats that your parents had to face while growing up. Just ask them about their greatest fears as teens. Every generation has its pandemics, wars, and worries. The difference today is the saturation of these fears and the ease with which teens can access the information contributes to anxiety.

Bringing Anxiety Down to a Manageable Level

When it comes to dealing with sudden anxiety that makes you experience fear in the moment—what professionals call "acute" anxiety—the most important thing to do is to bring the anxiety down. Remember, you can't make all of the anxiety go away. That's not your goal. In fact, making anxiety go away completely in these moments is impossible. Your goal is simply to bring the anxiety down to a more manageable level. You can do this using a set of skills called relaxation techniques.

You first need to make sure two things are happening:

1. You are in a safe place.
2. You are breathing evenly. The best way to do this is to breathe in for four seconds and out for four seconds (4x4 breathing). When breathing in, imagine the air filling in all the way to the bottom of your lungs.

Without these two steps in place, your anxiety will remain elevated, and the remainder of skills you review won't be as effective because your brain will be too preoccupied to focus on anything else. Please keep this in mind.

This is not about blame. This is about cause and effect. Pointing the finger and blaming (especially in a book) isn't helpful. Saying, "You do this to me!" does not fix the problem. What fixes the problem is personally working with your own feelings about the situation and determining why this particular issue is an issue for you. But if you are too activated, being this self-aware is impossible. So let's look at a specific skill to bring your attention to the present moment.

Let's start the process right now.

CATEGORIES

The first relaxation skill I'll describe is called "categories." This skill is particularly effective in dealing with seemingly impossible-to-get-rid-of crisis thoughts. You know, the ones that get you riled up in the moment, and that you can't stop thinking about. These are the types of thoughts for which categories are most effective.

The skill itself is relatively simple. Select any category, such as capital cities in the US, types of cereal, names of crayon colors by Crayola, countries in the world, names of actors, programming languages, etc., and list as many of these as you can. For example, if you were to select different types of breakfast cereals, you would then list as many different types that you are able. So, there's Frosted Flakes, Chex, Kix, Lucky Charms, Cheerios, Honey Nut Cheerios, Count Chocula, Rice Krispies, etc. List these items until you cannot come up with any more.

The first two to five items will be easy to recall. You will then start to struggle a bit to name a few more, and then the struggle is going to become more intense where it's harder to think of anything. You're going to say to yourself that you're done and can't think of any more. Don't stop because this is the important part! It's the point where you need to keep at it, because it's how you stop those troubling, anxious crisis thoughts. I cannot stress this enough. When the struggle is real, that's the time to push forward and add at least one, preferably three more items to that category. This is where your frontal lobe gets engaged, which helps to disrupt the anxious connection between your frontal lobe and the amygdala. You'll know you're there when the only thing you can think of is whatever the category is, and not what originally spiked your anxiety just moments before. The technique of categories is that simple.

The thing to remember when selecting a category is to choose something general enough to have many options, but not so general that it's not a challenge. When doing this, do your best to name as many as you're able.

In clinical sessions, I tell people not to worry about the number and do their best. It is typically around naming the 15th item within the category that their anxious thoughts fade away and they can only think of the category. The best part of this anxiety-reducing skill is that you can do it anywhere at any time.

ACTIVITY

Practicing Categories

Have a few categories ready to go the next time you begin feeling anxious. Come up with three categories here that you could name more than six items of, but that will also provide some difficulty.

1. _____

2. _____

3. _____

Recall that another symptom of anxiety is catastrophizing. It's a thinking error that happens when you convince yourself that in the moment, the situation is worse than it really is. Similar to catastrophizing is a thinking error called future tripping. This is when you think something in the future is going to be worse than the reality.

I want you to recognize when you start catastrophizing or future-tripping to remain in control of your thoughts. It's about taking a step back—and seeing your thoughts from an objective point of view. This helps to disrupt the errant belief that just because you think it, it must be true. Thoughts and emotions do not equal reality! Organizing your thoughts helps you to see the reality of the situation rather than the false construct that your anxiety is so adept at convincing you is true.

By the way, the goal here is to not lie to yourself. People sometimes get confused about this. There are scary and difficult things in life. This is a universal truth of being a human on this planet. But you only make things worse by catastrophizing the situation.

You feel worse because catastrophizing does two things:

1. It does not accept the reality of the situation. When you catastrophize, what you're really telling yourself is that you don't like or approve of the situation. This nonacceptance approach is guaranteed to make it worse because it makes you fight against reality. Unfortunately, reality wins every time.

2. It prevents you from solving the problem. When you tell yourself things are worse than they really are, it creates a sense of helplessness. Once you're in this state, it's easy to let your mind run with the fear, and it becomes more difficult to regain a sense of control. The all-important locus of control becomes external instead of internal. When you feel that you are in control of the situation, the helplessness will fade.

Catastrophizing can relate to any of a vast amount of worst-case scenarios, from an upcoming exam or class presentation to a playoff game or approaching a guy or girl you've liked since last summer. So how do you challenge the catastrophizing and regain your locus of control in these scary moments?

When you catastrophize, your thoughts stop at the point you believe is the worst-case scenario. You then obsess about this one moment, seeing it in the most awful way. You never think about what might happen right after that moment of your greatest fear. But you can train your mind to stop doing this by continually asking, "And what's so bad about that?"

Nothing in the affairs of men is worthy of great anxiety.

—Plato

For example, if you receive a poor grade at school, it's normal to experience all the feelings that go along with this result. But if you feel that your reaction is stronger than reality, applying the question, "And what's so bad about that?" is a great tactic.

ACTIVITY

Training Your Mind to Stop Catastrophizing

On a sheet of paper, write out your initial catastrophizing thought. It's always best to see these thoughts on paper and out of our minds. After you write down the thought, ask yourself, "What's so bad about that?" Write down your answer and repeat until you come to a calmer, more realistic answer.

So, it might look something like this:

You: "I got a bad grade. My parents are going to be so mad at me!"

"And what's so bad about that?"

You: "Well, I might get in trouble or be punished in some way. Or I'll fail at school."

"And what's so bad about that?"

You: "I don't want to get in trouble. And if I fail school, I'll never get into a good college and get a good job and … (Insert lengthy catastrophizing here!)"

Eventually the worst-case scenario becomes highly unrealistic and you will naturally start to challenge what you are writing down. In this example, that will look something like, "Is that really likely because of one bad grade?!"

You: "OK, I can see that's what is triggering my anxiety. But that's likely not going to happen."

WAYS TO ALLEVIATE ANXIETY

57. Question the validity of your anxiety. (Is this worry realistic? What's the worst that can happen? And what's so bad about that? Is this really true, or does it just seem that way?)

58. Put a piece of chocolate in your mouth and see how long you can keep it there before you bite into it.

59. Learn to throw a knuckleball or fast pitch a softball.

60. Throw a Frisbee with someone. It's both fun and cathartic.

61. Learn to drive a manual transmission (if you're old enough).

62. Learn how to do a handstand or cartwheel.

63. Implement some simple breathing exercises, like 4x4 breathing (see page 134).

64. Get busy. Do something—anything. Just stay in motion being productive, engaged in some form of self-care, being social, etc.

CHAPTER 9

CLIMATE CHANGE

I sure do love living on Earth. I hope no one ruins it by climate change.

Despite what those big oil commercials try to spin, the cause of climate change today is mostly due to humans burning fossil fuels for energy. In short, they're taking it out of the ground (where it should stay) and putting it into the atmosphere. This leads to increased levels of carbon dioxide in the atmosphere. No one asked them to, but big oil executives can't be bothered with silly things like a flammable planet and mass extinctions.

High levels of carbon dioxide in the atmosphere from fossil fuel use cause the Earth's temperature to increase. These changes are often referred to as "global warming." Climate change has also led to other extreme weather events such as destructive hurricanes, flooding, tornadoes, wildfires, severe winter storms, and comically large wide-brimmed sun hats.

If those who believe in climate change are wrong, numerous industries will have been required to develop cleaner alternatives without reason. If those who don't believe in climate change are wrong, we all die. So do the penguins and polar bears.

> *Earth is not a platform for human life. It's a living being. We're not on it but part of it. Its health is our health.*
> —Writer and poet Thomas Moore

Consider that prior to the 1960s, plastic straws weren't even a thing. Somehow people still enjoyed their venti caramel ribbon crunch Frappuccinos. And do rich folk know climate change will ruin their ski trips? You can't have après-ski with no snow. Have we exhausted this angle? In 2017 the American Psychological Association and ecoAmerica defined eco-anxiety as "a chronic fear of environmental doom."[1]

Feeling anxious is a completely appropriate response to the severity of climate change. It would be odd to not feel some anxiety about it. But it can manifest in troubling ways, such as obsessive thinking, sleep problems, or panic attacks. Your response to feeling eco-anxiety can include talking to a counselor regarding your concerns about the future, avoiding single use plastics, engaging in social activism, and calling out musicians and influencers who take private jets to brunch.

I should note that while writing this chapter, Elon Musk was called out for taking his private plane on a nine minute, 35-mile flight from San

---

1 S. Clayton et al., *Mental Health and Our Changing Climate: Impacts, Implications, and Guidance* (Washington, DC: American Psychological Association and ecoAmerica, 2017).

Jose to San Francisco, California—a daily commute by car or a mere five rail stops for millions of regular folk. Climate activism is associated with resilience and positive development but may also be a source of increased stress, particularly for marginalized youths. You can start some civic engagement with the Action for the Climate Emergency (ACE) team at AceSpace.org.

Person: "You're always so chill."
Me: "Yeah, well the anxiety literally paralyzes me so ..."

We agree that it's a scary time to be a teen. In fairness to our predecessors, it's always been a scary time to be a teen. Maybe you romanticize a prior era. Let's consider some recent epochs by way of comparison and to provide some perspective. We'll skip past the thousands of years back when life for most people was markedly short and rife with famine, disease, injury, and amputations, and when migraines were treated by drilling a hole into the skull with stone tools. We'll also bypass the Industrial Revolution, known for its child labor in filthy factories.

Let's also sidestep medieval Europe during the Black Death (aka, "the plague"), which killed up to 200 million people and reduced the world's population by 22 percent. And the depressing colonization of the Americas that decimated Native American tribal societies and cultures while leaving much of North America a dystopian wasteland. Then there were the hundreds of years of slavery and institutionalized racism that have left an indelible mark on not just the psyche of America, but also on the current state of race relations, inequalities, and subsequent mental health of Black America.

We should probably forego the first half of the 20th century on account of its immeasurable suffering and angst. This grim period is marked by the highest concentration of suffering and misery in all of human history, much of it due to political ideologies practiced within the span of only 30 years. It was a chaos casserole of all known human pain and suffering since the dawn of time neatly packed into one generation.

It began with World War I, the first technologically modern war that dished death and mayhem on previously unprecedented levels. Yay, technology.

If you somehow avoided becoming one of the 40 million casualties,[2] you could look forward to the war's end in 1918 and the start of the global Spanish Flu pandemic. It was a savage, angry flu strain that targeted young, healthy adults and killed about 100 million people. Those lucky enough to survive the war and pandemic were met with the dire poverty and unemployment of the Great Depression of the 1930s. Never before did society deserve a bigger break only to experience the start of World War II in 1939, leading to 15 million battle deaths and 45 million civilian deaths.[3] If you lost count, that's back-to-back-to-back-to-back bad mojo. Only it didn't stop there.

---

2 Nadège Mougel, "World War I Casualties," Reperes—Module 1–0 Explanatory Notes, 2011, http://www.centre-robert-schuman.org/userfiles/files/REPERES%20 –%20module%201-1-1%20-%20explanatory%20notes%20–%20World%20War %20I%20casualties%20–%20EN.pdf.

3 The National WWII Museum, New Orleans, https://www.nationalww2museum. org/students-teachers/student-resources/research-starters/research-starters -worldwide-deaths-world-war.

In the 1950s during the latter half of the 20th century, America slipped into the Korean War (which is technically ongoing), the start of the Cold War, and the domestic unrest of the civil rights movement. It offered only Elvis as a consolation. The world nearly ended in the 1960s with the Cuban Missile Crisis. It literally came down to the decision of a single human. Then America was served its first major war loss in Vietnam. And not even the hippies and all their free love and flower power could save America from the escalating racial strife and widespread riots that preceded and followed the Civil Rights Act of 1964.

The 1970s were fraught with the Watergate Scandal, when White House operatives were caught burglarizing the Democratic National Committee. It also marked the Three Mile Island nuclear accident in Pennsylvania. Meanwhile, women, African Americans, Native Americans, gays and lesbians, and other marginalized people continued their fight for equality, as the nation hit 14 percent inflation in a period called The Great Inflation. The decade also unleashed disco and *Jaws*—two distinct and forever haunting relics.

Before there were Instagram filters there was smog.

In considering the late 20th century, things weren't so great in hindsight either. The '80s remain popular, but there was no internet, social

THE TEEN ANXIETY GUIDEBOOK

media, cell phones, or comprehensive smog checks, all while grown men in mullets wore Day-Glo parachute pants and fanny packs. They drove Camaros and mini trucks with wink mirrors and ground effects neon lighting.

The '80s had the Cold War and the constant threat of a Russian incursion. When people weren't fearing a life of communism, they feared AIDS, which had no suitable treatment and struck horror among casual sex-goers. America had an actor for president and racism was casually accepted. It was also a lost decade for American cars. They were hideous and ate cassette tapes in the middle of your favorite song.

And the real kicker? People had to rent movies from stores that were always out of the best new releases. Society was collectively guilted into a "be kind, rewind" culture and often charged for the replacement of the VHS tapes when they were late. And there was no LGBTQ acronym, but there were U2 and the B-52's.

In closing out the 20th century, the '90s came with the Rwandan genocide, the Yugoslav Wars, the Oklahoma City and first World Trade Center bombings, the LA Riots, Columbine, the Gulf War, and ... "The

Macarena." And this era required that you kept a phone book to call your friends. People memorized phone numbers because they'd ultimately lose the book and have to wait to hear from BFs.

People lived primordially. Songs existed only on CDs, which would skip in portable CD players and cars with the slightest bump. And can you imagine needing to print lists of directions from the internet before you went somewhere, yet still getting lost? That's assuming you could use the internet, with family members disconnecting the modem by picking up the phone to get movie times or excitedly calling Fotomat to see if the film from the Depeche Mode concert two weeks prior had been developed.

The start of the 21st century had its own apocalyptic flair. Everyone thought the world would end at midnight on New Year's Eve when the computer clocks ticked from 1999 to 2000. Then 9/11 and years of unwinnable wars in Iraq and Afghanistan followed. The first decade of the 2000s brought us belly chains and low-rise jeans, a recession, a housing market crisis, the rise of Paris Hilton, Myspace, and the unfathomable death of Steve Irwin. Not even the cozy, enveloping hug of a wearable blanket with arms could save us. Thanks for nothing, Snuggie.

The preceding timeline serves only to bolster the argument that, though the current era seems especially problematic, it tracks with the anxieties of prior generations going back 200,000 years. Only the sets and subsets of problems and related anxieties have changed. Yet people are still around, and still feeling anxious about "uncertain times."

Today we all face the existential threat of climate change while feeling not just eco-anxious, but eco-angry ... even eco-rage. The anger is rooted in rightful feelings that former generations were abhorrent stewards of the planet, putting profits and short-term gains before this incredible orb. You're spot-on in demanding that more powerful actors take responsibility for stopping and reversing the damage.

> *Billionaires when you ask them to help with climate change:*
> *"Best I can do is rocket some friends and me to space."*

When thinking about climate change, you likely experience feelings of anxiety, anger, helplessness, and guilt. You might use a type of defiant hope where, rather than pessimism and hopelessness, you force yourself to feel some noncommittal optimism. Optimism isn't always a prelude to disappointment.

A research study performed in different countries showed that adolescents and emerging adults (ages 16 to 25) worry a lot about climate change and that they feel betrayed by the adult world concerning the problem.[4] As they should. You are not responsible for the current state of the world. But you are part of the generation poised to worsen

4 Maria Ojala, "How Do Children, Adolescents, and Young Adults Relate to Climate Change? Implications for Developmental Psychology," *European Journal of Developmental Psychology* (2022), https://doi.org/10.1080/17405629.2022 .2108396.

things through unsustainable actions, or assist in improving the world by acting in as climate-positive a manner as possible daily, influencing your parents and friends and applying pressure on politicians through political protest. Expressly the latter, since the biggest polluters are corporate lobbyists in the back pockets of your representatives.

The only time an animal should risk death from ingesting plastic is when it eats a person with implants.

It's easy to feel like climate change is too overwhelming, thereby creating a sense of total powerlessness like unless you stow away to Mars you'll be left behind to fossilize with all the RVs, vape pens, and iPhones. But it's not that black and white. And it often creates a situation where a false belief exists that unless everyone takes action, then what's the point? This is dangerous rationale that is associated with less engagement. There's a crucial sense of achievement and positivity when joining together and protesting in a collective way. And not in a vain "misery loves company" style.

The curious thing about the psychological threat of climate change is that it leads to declining mental health not only for those directly impacted, but also for those who experience it indirectly through media, education, and even discussions with friends and parents. I call this "anxiety by proxy." Anxiety is a contagion.

Coping with climate change includes an aspect called "positive reappraisal," which requires the ability to switch your perspective between focusing on dire potential outcomes related to the issue, and positive aspects like the fact that more and more people now take climate change seriously.

The takeaway here is that you play an important role in influencing the climate change interest and engagement of your friends. You are a powerful socialization agent regarding climate in motivating others to make behavioral changes locally and even globally. Your reach is formidable today via global social media platforms. And think of the joy you'll feel when birds returning from winter migration see their home hasn't been cut down. "Hello again, favorite branch. Chirp, chirp!"

It's true we have a satellite orbiting Jupiter, while major auto manufacturers down here have had functioning plans since the 1970s for engines that could run on renewable energy, but sequestered them in favor of internal combustion power. A clear instance of moving forward while in reverse.

But despite what you might feel, you are a unilateral force in righting the wrongs of governments and corporations. In fact, global organizations—and humanity in general—are relying on youth to persuade the masses. In short, you don't need to flex your favorite Armageddon outfit for the 'gram yet.

DR. TOM'S TAKE

STRATEGIES FOR MANAGING ECO-ANXIETY

By now, you've gleaned that every generation has experienced overwhelming challenges that appeared insurmountable and debilitating. And yet, they found a way. What you can take away from these historical experiences is a sense of hope. If previous generations have faced scary odds and survived, then you can as well. Hope isn't a strategy, so let's make some plans.

To that end, managing your anxiety around this issue is a necessary first step. We'll focus on a particular type of stress-management, called grounding skills, next.

GROUNDING SKILLS

Grounding skills are exercises you can do in the moment that help "ground" you to the present. Often they include relying on using the senses to help redirect your focus to what is happening in real time, right in front of you. Why is this helpful? By focusing on the present moment, you can reduce your stress. Most of the time being focused on the exact moment soothes us. In much the same way an athlete or performer takes a deep breath before they walk on the field or stage to clear the head. Soaring always starts from the ground.

TO DO LIST:

1. Live in the moment.
2. Return to step 1.

You might think that you already do this, and this exercise is a waste of your time. But ask yourself, "Am I really focusing on the exact moment, or am I actually in my head about something else?" If the goal is to help reduce anxiety, then the best and quickest option is to redirect your anxious thoughts about the future and become intensely curious or interested about the current moment. It doesn't have to be your favorite moment. But it can't be some future beach or eating ice cream moment. Unless you're at the beach eating ice cream at this moment. After bringing your anxiety down to a more manageable level, you'll be in a more helpful place to consider the issues that were worrying you in the first place.

◼ ACTIVITY ◼
The Body Scan: Calming the Issues in Your Tissues

I wish we could call these what they are: a vibe scan. Body scans typically work best from a seated position.

1. Aim for a comfortable and upright position, making sure you're neither rigid nor slouched over. Take a deep breath and close your eyes.

2. Bring your attention to your feet. Try to notice the sensation of what it feels like for your feet to be connected to the ground. If you can remove your shoes and socks, this works best. If not, that's okay too. Try to notice what sensations you feel in your feet. Is there more pressure in one area of your foot versus another?

3. Take another deep breath and move your attention upward to your lower legs. Do you feel anything in your calves or shins? Is there tension, relaxation, or some other sensation? Is your skin covered by clothing or can you feel the air freely? Don't try to change or create any sensation, just observe and notice.

4. Take another deep breath and move your attention to your upper legs. Try to notice what it feels like along your legs as you sit in the chair. Is there more pressure in one part of your leg over another? Is there more than one sensation?

5. Taking another deep breath, move your attention up to your abdomen. What do you notice? Is there more pressure along your waist? What do you notice in your stomach as you breathe in and out? What does your shirt feel like as you breathe?

6. Again move your attention to your chest and shoulders. What do you notice? Can you feel the air coming into your lungs with your breaths? Do you notice your shoulders moving up and down? Is there more pressure along one area over another? Again, don't try to force any sensation, just try to observe and notice.

7. Finally, move your attention to your head and face. What sensations do you notice? What does the air feel like in your nose as you breathe? Is your jaw clenched or relaxed? Is there tension around your eye or forehead? What does it feel like at the top of your head?

8. When you're ready, take one final deep breath in and open your eyes. Observe how you feel. Revel in your newfound chill.

USE YOUR OTHER SENSES TO COUNTER YOUR "SPIDEY SENSE" (AKA, ANXIETY)

We reviewed the body scan; now let's check in with your senses. Not your sense of humor, sense of balance, common sense, or sense of style—but the five senses. This grounding tactic relies on your primary senses to help you notice the present. All that's required is to take a moment and observe the following:

- 5 things you can see
- 4 things you can hear
- 3 things you can touch
- 2 things you can smell
- 1 thing you can taste

For this grounding method, your success is in the details. For each item, try to be as descriptive as possible. For example, don't just cite a "tree" and move on to another object you can see. Instead, try to notice a specific detail of a particular leaf on that tree. Such as the way the shades of color change along the leaf or what the edges and stem look like. Then move on to another object you can see, trying to be as specific as possible along the way. Don't just check the mental box acknowledging that you've read the terms and conditions. The little things slow us down enough to focus. That's the secret sauce.

Ice Cube Technique

When I drop an ice cube, I just kick it under the fridge where it disappears. This exercise is nearly as straightforward. Place an ice cube in your open palm and hold it in your hand as it begins to melt. (You might want to place a towel under your hand to catch the melted water). While the ice cube is melting, use your senses to notice the change. What does the ice cube first feel like in your hand? How does the feeling change over time? Do you notice anything else in other parts of your body as the ice cube melts? If you can, try to also observe the change in the ice cube's shape over time. Hold the ice cube in your hand until it entirely melts away (if you can!).

These are but a small sample of the different types of grounding skills that are available to help reduce anxiety in the moment. Try to experiment with each to see if you have a preference, or if some work better in certain situations. The more practiced you become with grounding skills, the easier it will be to have something "to do" when your worry thoughts become too overwhelming. If you're doing them right, you'll come away the master of your emotional domain.

65. Get outside or go to the window and look out at the horizon.

66. Try using an adult coloring book. They're pretty fun!

67. Learn to say hello in as many languages as you can.

68. Pop any bubble wrap that you have around your house. Try to take a deep breath after each pop.

69. Envision what your role model would tell you about how to cope with this moment.

70. Try dimming the lights of your room to provide a different stimulus.

71. Learn a magic trick with playing cards.

72. Teach your family dog (or pet) a new trick.

73. Try to garden outside. Or just get your hands dirty and pull up some weeds.

74. Try to find new music or a band you might like.

CHAPTER 10

ANTICIPATION OF SCHOOL SHOOTINGS

Sure, we'd love to stop mass shootings. But we must respect a poorly written constitutional amendment that refers to barely functioning muskets.

—Unknown

America will ban schools before it bans guns.

This shouldn't be a chapter. It shouldn't even be a thing. In the old days, schools would practice earthquake, tornado, and fire drills. Active shooter drills would've been a thing of a dystopian future.

And here we are, all dystopian.

We're not going to make this about politics, gun control, or the Second Amendment, though it's important to point out that when James Madison wrote the Second Amendment in 1791, "arms" consisted of Revolutionary-era, single-shot muskets. But kids shouldn't fear wearing light-up Skechers because of the risk of being spotted by a campus shooter.

We're also not going to open with grim statistics except for a lesser-known fact: according to the Centers for Disease Control and Prevention (CDC) guns are now the leading cause of death among American children and teens. We lead the world in this sadistic issue. It's not even a thing in other countries. We're all past numb from the prevalence. Sadly, most of the world has tuned out to our plight of mass shootings in general. It's simply considered "an American thing" by outsiders. Like, "Those silly Americans and their love of guns and lack of conflict resolution skills ..."

We've tried nothing, and we're all out of ideas.

How can we be the only nation on the globe where this regularly occurs, yet feign helplessness to stop it? When someone failed at using a shoe for a bomb on a plane, every airport in the nation made us remove our shoes. In all fairness, there was no "shoe lobby" to go against the footwear bias because shoes don't kill people; people kill people. Or something. Even the "school shooting" page of Wikipedia asks readers to "please help update this article to reflect recent events." Not even Wikipedia believes in our ability to fix ourselves.

When I was in school, bullying was almost part of the curriculum. The bullying I experienced even decades ago left an enduring mark on me. There was no shortage of adversaries at my school or at the other seven high schools in my district. But we used our fists, not guns. Only the gang members would pull a weapon, but rarely at school. There were the occasional knives, brass knuckles, and nunchucks, but everyone followed an implicit code. Our goal was enemy submission, not human sacrifice. We still had homework and soccer practice.

We weren't as impulsive either. No matter the fury, we knew the big fights had to go down after school and off campus. My high school was in a sketch neighborhood across from some railroad tracks. The tracks were unmonitored and a frontier of anarchy. That's where we drank, smoked, and fought after school. It was a callous landscape of dirt, rocks, and broken bottles. If you lost a fight, you'd also worry about hepatitis and gangrene.

Our fights never resolved anything, of course. They were the peak of the flows between the ebbs of male teen aggression. Oftentimes, kids would fight the same person on and off for years. But no one was foolish enough to bring an AR-15 to school and terminate those they disliked, along with indiscriminate others.

If a kid hits another kid with a stick, do you:

a) Give everyone sticks.

b) Give sticks to those kids particularly adept with sticks to defend everyone else.

c) Take away the stick.

The overriding anxiety felt by students and parents related to school shootings is "What if?" As in what if it happens to me, or my child, or a loved one? At the time of this writing there are 98,755 public schools: 13,477 middle schools, 2,500 junior high schools, and 23,900 secondary schools in the US.[5] Statistically speaking, even within the gun-nuzzling ethos of the United States, your chance of being directly affected by a school shooting are exceptionally low. Similarly, few of us will encounter a shark either. But the moment we wade into an ocean we're convinced that we'll be eaten by *Jaws*. Thank you, mass media.

And let's be clear—arming teachers as a solution is like giving mortars to kids because the stationary feature of these big guns will accommodate their smaller stature. It's asinine. But in absence of a near-term solution to school or mass shootings in general, we need to address the implied anxiety that is intensified by the relentless media coverage after each one. Not to negate the reality of mass shootings, but there is a perceived threat and anxiety created by our media exposure.

According to research, news can fundamentally affect our emotional, cognitive responses and perceptions about the world. Exposure to the news is associated with anxious reactions and a perception that the world is far more dangerous than it is. Studies have also shown that repeated exposure to media violence creates a desensitizing effect as kids get older, thereby reducing fears and anxious reactions.[6] This is

5 Matthew Lynch, "Number of Schools in the U.S.," October 18, 2022, The Edvocate, https://www.theedadvocate.org/number-of-schools-in-the-u-s/#:~:text =The%20U.S.%20has%2098%2C755%20public,schools%20were%20available %20in%202018.

6 Gyo Hyun Koo, "Are You Frightened? Children's Cognitive and Affective Reactions to News Coverage of School Shootings," Mass Communication and Society, November 30, 2021, https://doi.org/10.1080/15205436.2021.1996609.

not the type of "exposure therapy" we want or recommend. Each of us needs to be a steadfast gatekeeper to our own psyche and mental well-being.

NO NEWS IS GOOD NEWS

My own parents watch the news on repeat throughout the day and evening. They have every upbeat streaming option available to them, but oddly choose news. When I've commented on the negative saturation, their reply is that it doesn't affect them, as if they're the winners of some case study in media desensitization. I don't believe them for a second. And why risk a permanent lower disposition at all? I won't be in the same room with them while soaking in the pessimism for hours a day when visiting. The news is a thief of joy.

The media is in the triggering business. Even their trigger warnings are made to amp the anticipation, garner views, sell advertising, and increase their business. Media execs aren't the least concerned with avoiding your negative emotions based on excessive reporting of shooting suspects or presenting graphic portrayals of an incident. Keep in mind there are people trying to improve things, however. And our collective resistance and resilience will ultimately win out. But regularly digesting news media is like a constant pessimism drip. If someone followed you around 24/7 saying, "I have more bad news for you ..." you'd sprint from them.

The only social benefit I can think of to broadcasting gruesome, unbalanced media coverage of school shootings is to rile us up enough to demand change. But it leaves the traumatic collateral damage of anxiety and fear in a wide wake. Traumas negatively affect developing brain structures of teens, which can lead to long-term problems.[7] If you are constantly exposed to negative news, experience emotional disturbances, and live with distrust or anxiety about the world, it can trap you in a vicious cycle of doom and hopelessness.

Studies show that school mass shootings are associated with various adverse psychological outcomes (e.g., post-traumatic stress disorder [PTSD], fear, stress, anxiety, depression, and substance use) both in the immediate aftermath and long term.[8] But you don't need a study to prove this. Each shooting creates concentric circles of trauma. The suffering and distress starts with the victims and resonates outward until it impacts the psyches of those thousands of miles away who see or read the news. Collectively, we're all victims.

---

7 R. Hariman and J. L. Lucaites, "Public Identity and Collective Memory in U.S. Iconic Photography: The image of 'Accidental Napalm,' *Critical Studies in Media Communication* 20, no. 1 (October 2010), 35–66, https://doi.org/10.1080 /0739318032000067074.

8 S. Lowe and S. Galea, "The Mental Health Consequences of Mass Shootings," *Trauma, Violence & Abuse 18*, no. 1 (January 2017): 62–82, https://doi.org/10.1177 /1524838015591572.

The accountability falls to everyone. If you see something troubling on social media, if you see someone getting bullied, if you hear threats being made—even as a joke—or if you have a chance to make contact with another kid on the fringe who has been sidelined or socially banished by their peers, reach out. You don't have to become best friends, but it comes down to basic humanity. If you think it will diminish your status among peers, don't. Standing up for someone in need is the most reputable and trending thing you can do. Now more than ever a simple, "Hey, you doing okay?" can save lives and make you a fast hero.

In four out of five school shootings, at least one other person had knowledge of the attacker's plan but failed to report it.[9] And nearly all mass school shooters shared threatening or concerning messages or images. More than 75 percent raised concern from others prior to the attacks, and bystanders saw warning signs in most documented active shooter cases.[10]

The typical school shooting cycle plays out as such:

Shooting ⇨ "Thoughts & prayers" ⇨ Online debates ⇨ Congress does nothing ⇨ Everyone but the victims' families forgets ⇨ *crickets* ⇨ Repeat …

Even God long ago said, "Truly I tell you, whatever you did for one of the least of these brothers and sisters of mine, you did for me." We can start by being nicer to one another. Since God helps those who help themselves, let's assume he too has grown weary of "thoughts and prayers" in place of actual legislation.

Rather than retroactive platitudes on the back end, let's proactively reach out to people on the front end before things go awry. Reach out

---

9 B. Vossekuil, R. Fein, M. Reddy, R. Borum, and W. Modzeleski, *The Final Report and Findings of the Safe School Initiative* (Washington, DC: US Secret Service and Department of Education, 2004).

10 U.S. Secret Service National Threat Assessment Center, *Mass Attacks in Public Spaces: 2019* (Washington, DC: Department of Homeland Security, 2020).

to the outliers, the misfits, the loners, and the bullied while extending some humanity. It works. Oftentimes it's the kid everyone predicted would do something. There were red flags, complaints, warnings, and derelict parents. Then … there was access to a gun.

What does not work is retroactivity. Consider the evidence:

1. The United States government budgets approximately one trillion dollars a year for military and police spending in order to protect the country and its citizens from undue harm.[11] Yet despite this colossal investment in "defense," the primary cause of death for children and adolescents in the US is a gunshot.

2. Security measures like active shooting drills, police response, armed campus security officers, etc., are reactionary and never meant to prevent a shooting, only to slow or eventually stop one that has begun. There is little or no evidence indicating that these reactionary policies have any effect on reducing school shootings.[12]

Research further advocates that schools expand access to counseling, increase training of school personnel on threat assessment and mental illness, use interdisciplinary threat assessment teams, monitor and follow up on treatment plans, expand involuntary treatment, implement bullying prevention, and increase interdisciplinary communication.[13]

Q: How many members of Congress does it take to change a lightbulb?
A: More guns.

I live in Northern California and I've had two knives and a gun pulled on me in my young life. All were incidents where I pursued someone

---

11 P. Reeping, "School Shootings Are Preventable, Not Inevitable," *BMJ* (2022): 377, https://www.bmj.com/content/377/bmj.o1378.

12 P. Reeping, "School Shootings Are Preventable."

13 S. Gregory and J. Park, "Mass School Shootings: Review of Mental Health Recommendations," *School Mental Health* 14, no. 3 (September 2022): 640–54.

out of the liquor store at which I worked, when they stole something and I gave chase. I was 18 and don't recommend working at a liquor store in a sketch area. Or chasing thieves. I quickly stopped when a weapon was pulled. I wasn't going to die over a carton of Marlboro's or fifth of gin.

I didn't feel immediate fear in those instances due to the adrenaline and surrealism of the situations. I felt rage. I felt a fury of powerlessness against the cowards who knew I was unarmed and 160 pounds soaking wet. And I later felt grateful that I wasn't stabbed or shot. The fear and anxiety came later.

Tom and I certainly don't propose to lessen incidents of mass and school shootings via a book chapter. We do, however, want to lessen your stress, worry, and anxieties related to the fear of a potential school shooter.

DR. TOM'S TAKE

WHAT TO DO IN LIGHT OF THE EXISTING GUNPOWDER AROMATHERAPY

The following skills are designed to help with anticipatory anxiety about school shootings. Or to put it another way, we want to bring the anxiety down to a more helpful level. The goal is not to remove all anxiety about school shootings. That would be unreasonable. It's normal and healthy to have some anxiety about this issue. We just don't want it to be overwhelming or get in the way with the rest of your life.

A note on anticipatory anxiety. Similar to Chapter 8 "Anxiety Related to the Future," anticipatory anxiety is what occurs when we feel anxious waiting for something to happen. As a result, when we are anticipating something, we feel out of control. We feel as though this ominous, terrible thing is going to happen and there's nothing we can do. We feel helpless.

Knowing this, the goals of these skills are to increase your sense of control and remind you that you are not helpless.

DAILY HABITS

One of the most foundational practices you can do to reduce anxiety is practicing healthy daily habits. What do we mean by this? Creating good routines around sleep, exercise, and diet is extremely important in managing your anxiety. We can't emphasize this enough.

So if you're feeling overwhelmed thinking about school shootings, the first thing you should do is check in with yourself and see if sleep, exercise, or diet has been different the last couple of days. Here are some guidelines to help inform you:

Diet: There is an overwhelming amount of information on the internet about how to eat healthfully. For purposes of managing your mental health, we suggest simply ensuring you do not overeat, under eat, or eat too many processed foods. Natural foods don't cause people to die from natural causes. Processed foods do. If your food can go bad, it's good for you. If your food can't go bad, it's not good for you.

Sleep: Insomnia is often the act of replacing sleep with anxiety. The Mayo Clinic suggests that teens receive 8 to 10 hours of sleep per night. We'd like to stress that it also helps to wake up at the same time every day, including weekends. This sets your internal clock and makes it easier to fall asleep around the same time each night. Staying up till 2 a.m. is self-destructive. Additionally, if you're struggling with sleep, avoid looking at a screen an hour before bed. Reading a book, listening to calming music, drawing, or meditating are all great options.

Exercise: Some type of exercise that occurs for 30 minutes, five days per week is important. Keep in mind, this does not have to be particularly strenuous. You don't need to smash arms so hard you can't wash your hair. Anything that gets your heart rate up and causes you to start sweating counts. If you're not already doing this in PE or through after school activities, try to make time in your schedule.

"Y'all got any more of that BDNF?"

Adapted PE specialist, teacher, certified youth fitness coach, parent, and founder of Modi-fit.com Jared Sellers emphasizes fitness and sports movements as an effective tool to reduce anxiety and boost mental health. Fitness and motor movements allow kids to self-regulate feelings of anxiety and depression, while adding overall strength and fitness.

"My own son initially struggled in grade school and was diagnosed with anxiety. My wife and I got him engaged in regular outdoor endeavors like mountain biking, skiing, and school sports as a component in treating his anxiety. Not only did it lessen his anxiety, but he gained measurable confidence. Moreover, he better connected with peers and social groups through the increased access to sports and activities," says Sellers.

There's something important at play here called brain-derived neurotrophic factor (BDNF). This is a powerful, exercise-produced growth factor that aids in the repair of brain cells, improves memory, increases growth of new brain cells, and more. It's truly a humble, heroic substance in our heads.

Physical exercise increases BDNF expression in the brain while providing other benefits to include the following: improving memory, preventing the development of Alzheimer's disease, regulating the function of the hippocampus, and decreasing insulin resistance and the prevention of diabetes and obesity. The enhanced brain BDNF levels that follow exercise even have a clinical improvement on depression.[14]

Conversely, decrease in the expression of BDNF is seen in many neurological diseases such as Alzheimer's disease, Parkinson's disease, Huntington's disease, and bipolar disorder.[15] BDNF levels increase with regular bouts of exercise. In fact, many researchers now believe that regular exercise is the single best way to produce BDNF to naturally alter mood and reduce anxiety. This kind of makes you your own moving, happiness factory.

Sellers recommend the following to all ages and fitness levels when starting a fitness program:

- Keep it simple and attainable. When starting with a new exercise routine, start with simple body weight movements. Choose four or five full body exercises that can be repeated (in a circuit), and that are easily completed in a short amount of time. Using little or no equipment at the outset is better for newbies. You can add weight or equipment later. If you think a minute goes by fast, try planking for one. Focus on

---

14 S. Bathina and U. Das, "Brain-Derived Neurotrophic Factor and Its Clinical Implications," *Archives of Medical Science* 11, no 6, (2015): 1164–78.

15 Bathina and Das, "Brain-Derived Neurotrophic Factor."

achieving short-term goals via short workouts. These will grow into larger achievements as you gain strength, endurance, and understanding.

- Allow for choice. Create a list of sports, exercises, and activities that you enjoy or have always wanted to try. "I often see kids in middle and high school dragging their feet at PE or constantly making excuses for lack of engagement. If they have more choice in what the activity is, the more likely they will work hard and come back for more," says Sellers. Think team sports versus burpees.

- Write it down. Commit to journaling or keeping a log of the activity or exercise for the first 30 days. This can be a small calendar printout posted on the wall of the garage or hallway with check marks, or forging your progress into stone tablets using steel and your newfound muscles. Seeing the completed work in a visual format over a month can be a powerful reinforcer and adds to a sense of accomplishment and motivation.

- Invite a friend or family member to join the activity. Research shows you are more likely to continue to work out with the support of a friend or family member. For young people struggling with anxiety, having a trusted friend involved will ease the challenge of trying something new.

- Modify as necessary. Modifications that increase intensity take consideration and care. One of the best modifications is simply to work at a more intense rate. This may be by adding speed, extending time, or increasing resistance. The goal is to safely build up the intensity over short periods while working toward your overall goals. Life doesn't get easier, you get stronger.

REDUCE THE AMOUNT OF SCHOOL SHOOTING CONTENT YOU CONSUME

It's important to stay informed, but too much of anything can be problematic. This is especially true if you are consuming school shooting media and have anxiety symptoms. We know it might seem counterproductive to consume less media around shootings. It might even feel like the more informed you are about these events, the lower your anxiety. Long term, however, it's likely you will worsen your anxiety by regularly consuming threatening news. Why?

Let's revisit the anxious brain from Chapter 1. The amygdala (located in the middle of your brain, one in each hemisphere) is central to your anxiety response. Think of it as a power source that keeps anxiety going. Whereas the frontal lobe is the more thoughtful, thinking part of our brain. The frontal lobe slows down anxiety. In essence, the amygdala is the "gas," and the frontal lobe is the "brake." Which one comes out ahead and releases the chill is largely based on your actions.

When you overconsume threatening news, you reinforce and strengthen the amygdala. It can actually grow in size over time! More gas and less brake. This is why people become more fearful over time as they consume threatening news or are exposed to other threatening triggers. By focusing too often on school shootings, your brain is "triggered" and exposed to a threat. Whereas when you reduce how often you expose the brain to this threat, your amygdala will be less activated over time. Limiting exposure—so hot right now.

There was a study conducted by the National Institutes of Health on anxious teens that were exposed to media after the Boston Marathon Bombings. Researchers found that "media exposure may be particularly likely to trigger PTSD symptoms in youths with high physiological reactivity to stress." Essentially, they found that if you are already an anxious teen, watching too much news about traumatic events is one of the variables that can contribute to PTSD. Keep in mind these teens were not at the bombings, they were just watching too much coverage. You can never watch too much good news or cat videos, however.

BE PROACTIVE, NOT PASSIVE

A common theme in this book is recognizing that avoidance makes anxiety worse. When we avoid a perceived threat we are unconsciously giving control of ourselves to that threat. Similar to a pinball that gets knocked around by the machine, we feel out of control and at the mercy of that threat. Psychologists call this an external locus of control. An external locus of control is when we perceive something outside of ourselves that has an overwhelming influence over our lives. Something else is controlling our destiny instead of ourselves.

It's human nature to default to the path of least resistance. But your goal is to flip this perspective and create an internal locus of control. An internal locus of control occurs when you feel like you have more influence over your life. You feel more in charge of your destiny. So how do you apply this understanding to anxiety about school shootings? Be proactive.

Here are some examples of what being proactive looks like:

- Reaching out to your elected official and asking what steps they are taking to solve this issue.

- Talking to teachers or school administrators about your concerns.
- Being informed of your school's active shooter drills.
- Volunteering with local organizations that are associated with the issue.
- Searching for fundraising opportunities such as a local walk/ 5k run.
- Visiting the Sandy Hook Promise website at www .sandyhookpromise.org for more proactive opportunities.

REINFORCE POSITIVE SCHOOL EXPERIENCES

When trying to help with school shooting anxiety it's important to focus on the positive experiences at school as well. Similar to other stress management techniques in this book, bringing your focus to nonthreatening events helps to reduce anxiety overall.

In Chapter 12 we discuss mental filters. An additional mental filter not mentioned in that chapter is "Disqualifying the Positives." Often this filter is associated with depression, but it's also relevant to this issue. When we adopt a Disqualifying the Positives mentality, we are closing ourselves off to experiences or evidence that makes us feel less threatened or sad about a situation. It's not about manifesting things or dismissing real threats or events; it's about allowing ourselves to recognize positive experiences happen in schools as well.

If you find yourself disqualifying or ignoring positive experiences at school, then you would likely benefit from this exercise discussed in Chapter 12.

1. Write out the disqualifying positive thought.
2. Write out a challenge to this thought.

For example:

Disqualifying the Positives Thought: I can't go to school. Nothing good happens there.

Challenge: Yes, I do feel scared, and that's normal. But I'm taking steps to help with this. And some good things happen at school.

Getting in a habit of using this exercise daily can help improve how you handle thoughts that are overly negative about school.

TALKING TO A PROFESSIONAL

If you feel like your anxiety about school shootings is too overwhelming and it is getting in the way of the rest of your life, then it's best to talk to your parents or a teacher about meeting with a mental health professional. While the information in this book is meant to help, it is not meant to be a replacement for treatment. School shootings are traumatic, and any anxiety related to them is normal and deserving of help.

WAYS TO ALLEVIATE ANXIETY

75. Take a cold shower.

76. Invite a friend over to watch a comedy movie.

77. Learn to crochet.

78. Spend some time with your family pet.

79. Make a playlist of songs you like and plan to share it with a friend.

80. Shoot some hoops.

81. Use your phone to identify the constellations of the stars at night.

82. Make yourself a smoothie.

83. Complete a crossword puzzle.

84. Wrap a cold washcloth over your forehead for five minutes.

CHAPTER 11

ANXIETY AND SUBSTANCE ABUSE

There's not a drug on Earth that can make life meaningful.

—Sarah Kane

RISKY BUSINESS

Though today I exhibit some OCD characteristics and am regarded as a very hygienic man, when I was a child, the parents of other children often wondered if I had a home—or even a legal guardian. I would spend school recesses launching myself off jungle gyms into tanbark and dirt. On rainy days, I was consistently sent home by school administrators for a change of clothing due to romps in the mud. I also habitually feigned illness so I could remain home from school, where I would burn things, including my plastic toys. I savored the sight of black, noxious smoke spiraling into the sky. On the weekends, playing with friends was akin to hours of dust bathing. We played mud football, stole things, scaled trees and rooftops, climbed under vehicles, foraged for scorpions and lizards, and swam in the local squalid rivers and creeks while dining upon their bountiful harvest of crayfish that we would catch using only string and chicken liver for bait. I'm the reason I don't have a boy of my own.

The sole dirty habit I missed as a child was smoking, but not for lack of trying. Fortunately, I also lacked opportunity. But the "opportunity" manifested itself haplessly one afternoon. I was footloose and shuffling down the street from my house when a salty, grizzled old woman drove past me squinting from decades of defending smoke entrails from her tear ducts. She tossed a smoldering 2-inch cigarette butt from her car window. I dashed across the street to the glowing nub and grasped it between thumb and forefinger. It was macabre in appearance—a brown-tinged cotton filter and pink lipstick prints encircling the end. Sadly, that hardly dissuaded my prepubescent mind from such a long-awaited toke. I violated far more than the seven-second rule when I raised the butt to my lips and took a deep drag into my virgin lungs. My body swiftly coughed and retched. I hurled the butt to the asphalt while gagging to expunge the toxic soot from my little chest. Fortunately, the memory stayed with me, and I find cigarettes vile today.

Nine out of ten people who meet the clinical criteria for substance abuse disorders involving nicotine, alcohol, or other drugs began smoking, drinking, or using before they turned 18. And consider this startling piece of data: Childhood anxiety disorders have been linked to early drug use.

As Dr. McDonagh explains in Risky Behavior: Alcohol, Drugs, and Driving (page 180), many people with anxiety try to make themselves feel better with drugs or alcohol. According to Adolescent Substance Abuse,[16] teen users are at significantly higher risk of developing an addictive disorder compared to adults, and the earlier they begin using, the higher their risk. According to a Columbia University study, people who begin using any addictive substance before age 15 are

---

16 Mark Garofoli, "Adolescent Substance Abuse," *Primary Care* 47, no. 2 (June 2020): 383–94, https://doi.org/10.1016/j.pop.2020.02.013.

six-and-a-half times as likely to develop a substance use disorder as those who delay use until age 21 or older (28.1 percent vs. 4.3 percent).

WHAT CAME FIRST, THE SUBSTANCE ABUSE OR THE ANXIETY?

Researchers have done many studies concerning this question. One worth noting was conducted by investigators Alexandra Wang and Dr. Delos Reyes at Case Western Reserve University, School of Medicine in Cleveland, Ohio. The study was done to determine links between anxiety and substance use, and which disorder starts first in teenagers. They found that the drug most often used in relation to anxiety disorders was marijuana. Of the 195 study participants, 92 percent had marijuana dependence. The researchers reported that 61 percent were alcohol dependent, having started to drink at 13.5 years on average. Teens with either social anxiety disorder or panic disorder were significantly more likely to have marijuana dependence. Additionally, panic disorder tended to start before alcohol dependence, occurring in 75 percent of alcohol-dependent adolescents.

HOW ARE THESE STATISTICS RELEVANT TO YOU?

It's impactful because those of us who suffer from any form of anxiety have a considerably elevated risk for substance abuse. If you're aware of your predisposition for substance use and abuse, you can head off potential disaster. Thinking of throwing back a few drinks at a party this weekend? Reconsider. The risk to you is far greater than that of your non-anxious peers. Alcohol and other substances can make your anxiety symptoms far worse because they can easily become an addiction for you. According to the Anxiety and Depression Association of America (ADAA), "People with anxiety disorders are two to three times more likely to have an alcohol or other substance abuse disorder at some point in their lives than the general population." I know I'm not painting an inspiring picture of anxiety and addiction. That's my intent. You need to know the dark reality about the relationship between anxiety and substance abuse. In addition to anxiety predisposing you to substance use, there's an inverse relationship to consider: Some drugs can actually make you more anxious, to include increased withdrawal, agitation, and even paranoia. Good times, eh?! Alcohol or drugs may temporarily relieve the distress of an anxiety disorder, but ultimately these substances only intensify the symptoms of anxiety.

Decades of research in psychiatry have shown that anxiety disorders and substance abuse occur at much greater rates than would be expected by chance alone. This is often referred to as "co-occurrence," where you have both anxiety and substance abuse happening. Now, add the complex teenage brain into the equation and things get really interesting. First, consider that our brains don't fully mature until at least age 25. Even without an anxiety disorder, while the brain is developing, teenagers are vulnerable to an array of risks and risky predilections where substance abuse and addiction are just one. The evolving teen brain is a strange and marvelous gelatinous entity. It simply doesn't weigh consequences the same as the adult version. Teenagers cannot exercise full control over impulses, leading to a greater risk for bad decisions, substance use, and addiction.

Most people with alcohol/substance use issues and anxiety disorders experience them separately, where the symptoms of one intensify and worsen the other. Having both is a risky progression that causes a downward cycle. For example, anxiety can lead someone to using alcohol or other substances in an attempt to self-medicate or lessen undesirable symptoms. But the substance use actually worsens both the anxiety and the symptoms, perpetuating the cycle. It's an "adding injury to injury" type of scenario.

I want to emphasize that if you never take the first you will never take the second. You will never become an alcoholic or addict.

—N. Eldon Tanner

I never really understood anxiety in my teens, or that the large percentage of my bad decisions, including alcohol abuse, was perpetuated by anxiety. After trying a few substances, I settled on alcohol as my go-to drug. Alcohol became my mind-bending substance of choice, and the only way to get booze in my early teens was to steal it. I stole it from family, neighbors, parties, and grocery/liquor stores. You'd think after my first few times puking from liquor that I'd avoid it. Sometimes I'd even puke 'n' rally, like while attending large events where I'd sneak away to vomit in someone's azalea bush, then restart drinking to drown the social anxiety into hazy submission. I often drank as if I'd never get a hold of alcohol again—but I always did.

> *Don't let your anxiety turn you into a person you are not—like a jerk or an addict.*

I hated most forms of alcohol the first 20 or so times I drank them. It makes no sense that I continued using it, which is often how substance abuse works. I noticed that despite sometimes making me sick, it also soothed what ailed within me. I became a home mixologist, learning to skillfully balance the prescription drugs and alcohol, never drinking too much too close to anxiety drug or sleeping pill dosing time. So I thought. In regular lapses of logic, I took them concurrently, even as many celebrities were making headlines dying in cheap motel rooms from similar moments of high anxiety.

Sadly, with alcohol on board, I never gave my meds a chance to work because in my amateur assessment, they never worked fast or well enough. My brain chemistry was like a simmering cauldron of crazy-stew. Every prescription bottle warned against drinking alcohol while taking the medicine. I'd like to tell you how many things went sideways during my days of alcohol-pill cocktailing, but the list is too long to recount. It saddens me that I abused a substance and myself for so long. I used alcohol as a complement to get over the humps. What small, temporary benefits I obtained with alcohol were met with far more devastation from increased anxiety, depression, and adverse events, like regret.

> *You were given this life because you are strong enough to live it.*

Let's consider your love of freedom and drive-thrus. Even without adding a substance, teen driving statistics are grim. Your parents are freaked out for good reason, because car crashes are a leading cause of death for teens, and about 25 percent of those crashes involve an underage, drinking driver.

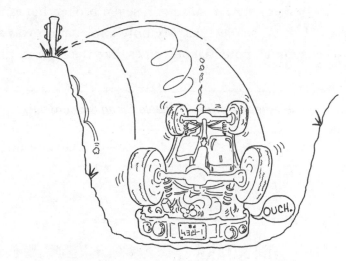

Teen driving is perilous enough without all the distractions beyond substance use, like teen passengers and texting. Researchers have found that young drivers are more likely to make risky decisions if their friends are present. For teen drivers, the risk of a crash doubles with just one extra passenger. In the order of things your parents worry about concerning you, it's driving responsibly, grades, social media, tsunamis, cobras, and pedophiles in Sprinter vans.

Driving instructor: "What do you do at a red light?" Teen driver: "I usually respond to texts and check my Instagram."

When I was a teen driver, I didn't have a phone, but I had a misfiring, impulsive brain that made me a rolling menace. I regularly drove my muscle car at 120 to 140 mph and my motorcycle at 160 mph on open freeways. I would never take these risks with my current, prudent brain. My risky driving behavior culminated in rolling my truck into an irrigation ditch when I was 18. My buddy and I were driving home from Taco Bell through farmland in Central California one Saturday afternoon when he abruptly dared me to take the next rural left turn as fast as I could in my pickup. Not one to shun a senseless taunt, or appear a coward, I took the dare. Though I changed my mind as we slid sideways off the road, catching air and landing upside down in a muddy ditch eight feet below, resulting in seven broken bones, lacerations, and a concussion between us. My only explanation was a brain that failed to consider all potential outcomes, like the rules of physics.

> *Hardships often prepare ordinary people for an extraordinary destiny.*
>
> —C. S. Lewis, author

DR. TOM'S TAKE

DRUGS ARE BAD, M'KAY?

A quick note: Jon's and my goal for this chapter is to inform and increase your awareness. It's not a scare tactic. We want it to be an easy reference for you to make an informed decision. However, it is only one, brief chapter. We barely scratch the surface of this issue. If you want to look for more, we suggest starting at the National Institute on Drug Abuse (NIDA; www.DrugAbuse.gov).

RISKY BEHAVIOR: ALCOHOL, DRUGS, AND DRIVING

So, why would a book on anxiety include a chapter about alcohol and drug use? As you can probably guess, more than a few people with anxiety try to make themselves feel better using drugs or alcohol. In 2011, Columbia University's National Center on Addiction and Substance Abuse found the following:

In general, for teenagers with and without anxiety or mental health issues:

○ 85 percent will experiment with drugs or alcohol.

- 15 percent will develop problems with drugs or alcohol.
- 10 percent will develop abuse or dependence problems with drugs or alcohol.

For those with mental health issues:

- 60 percent to 70 percent of people with a substance abuse problem also have another mental health diagnosis (like anxiety). Having both of these issues is called a dual diagnosis.

Why does this matter for teenagers? Because most of these mental health disorders first appear in adolescence or in young adulthood.

- One half have an onset before age 15.
- Three quarters have an onset before age 24.

SO WHAT'S THE BIG DEAL?

Well, if you are someone with a mental health diagnosis (like anxiety), then you have a greater chance of developing a drug or alcohol problem. This doesn't mean that anxiety will automatically make you have a substance abuse issue. Far from it. As Jon discussed, there is a definitive overlap between using substances and mental health problems. Anxiety is tough enough; adding an alcohol or drug problem just makes it harsher. Research presented by ABC News revealed the following:

"Sixteen-year-olds are three times more likely to have an accident than 18- or 19-year-olds, and eight times as likely as 25-year-olds. A young driver is involved in a fatal crash every 62 minutes, and car accidents are the leading cause of death for 15- to 20-year-olds. A survey in Southern California found that more than 70 percent of teen drivers in San Diego, Orange, and Los Angeles counties said they had been involved in drunken driving, drag racing, or other reckless driving behavior. Doctors say that 16—the traditional driving age in most states—may be the worst age to give children their driver's licenses, because at that age, they are often in the middle of a growth spurt in which their bodies grow faster than their central nervous system."

According to the Insurance Institute for Highway Safety, in the United States, the fatal crash rate per mile driven for 16- to 19-year-olds is nearly 3 times the rate of drivers ages 20 and over. Risk is highest at ages 16 to 17. In fact, the fatal crash rate per mile driven is nearly twice as high for 16- to 17-year-olds as it is for 18- to 19-year-olds.

Car accidents are a leading cause of teenage deaths.

SELF SCREENING

Let's say you fall into the majority—the 85 percent of teenagers who will experiment with drugs or alcohol. How do you know if this is something that is somewhat "normal" or something more serious that needs to be addressed? A fast and reliable way to make the determination is to go online to CRAFFT.org and complete the CRAFFT test. It's a quick screening test related to adolescent substance abuse, composed of six simple "yes" or "no" questions, where two or more "yes" answers suggest that you are at high risk.

If you learn that you're at high risk, then I suggest that you reach out to someone you trust to help you get in touch with a professional. Or, if that's not a comfortable option for you, contact any local health clinic yourself. Just because you're a teenager doesn't mean you can't take charge of your own well-being! There are always people that want to help you.

BASIC BIOLOGY OF RISKY BEHAVIOR

So, if there's such a risk involved in using substances (or any risky behavior), why do teenagers do it? Well, this is largely due to the fact that these risky behaviors make the moment feel good. It works in the short term. Now, in the long term, it isn't such a great solution, but as a teenager, you're not always thinking so far into the future. Especially when the right opportunity presents itself. The thinking of a teenager is much more in the "now." Adults have risky-behavior thoughts as well, but they tend to think more into the future. Adults will think more about the consequences of doing a risky thing. And this type of thinking, where there is a focus on the consequences, typically prevents adults from being more impulsive.

Why is there a difference in the thinking of teenagers versus adults? The answer is in the way our brains develop as we age. Remember the frontal lobe? The front of the frontal lobe is a smaller area called the prefrontal cortex. This smaller piece is where your advanced thinking occurs. It influences your personality, thinking about the future, and your ability to tolerate impulses. But your emotions, which start the impulses, come from the middle of the brain.

During your teen years the connection between the front of your brain and the middle of your brain is weak and still in development. As a result, when there are intense emotions, the prefrontal cortex isn't as connected, resulting in teens acting on the emotions without caring about future consequences. Have you ever said something while caught up in the moment, and then regretted it immediately after? That's what happens when your prefrontal cortex isn't as well connected to the middle part of your brain.

Thankfully, over time there is a fine tuning and strengthening of the connection between these parts of the brain. If you want to know more about this, there is a great paper from the National Institute of Health to check out: "The Adolescent Brain," written by B.J. Casey, Rebecca M. Jones, and Todd A. Hare.

FACE YOUR FEELINGS

If you stop and think about it, the impulsive feelings that get you into trouble don't just turn on at full force immediately. There is always a buildup process. Sometimes this buildup is long, sometimes it's a bit shorter. When you suddenly become aware of this feeling as it's building and tell yourself it's too much, that it'll never end, that's when you engage in the behavior that gets you into trouble. Maybe it's a feeling of boredom when driving, so you start to go faster. Or, maybe it's feeling intensely angry at someone, so you yell at them. There are many ways in which your impulsive feelings challenge you. But you only engage in the problematic behavior because you want to end the impulsive feeling. You're trying to do something to make the feeling go away. And that's the problem, because instead of making the feeling go away, you want to actually face it.

In the moment, you may believe strong feelings will never end, but that's not true. (Fun fact: The word "emotion" is based on the Latin word emovere, which means to move). Feelings, much like a wave, start out small, build in intensity, and then eventually fade. Now, maybe the feeling will go up and down like a series of waves for a while, but it will always go down.

Urge Surfing

While there is some biological explanation as to why we act more on our impulses when we are teenagers, it doesn't give you a hall pass to do whatever you want. The brain is pretty amazing, so with a little training, you can learn ways to reduce impulsive behavior. The trick for this is a skill called urge surfing.

The way to urge surf is to sit down (if possible), slowly breathe (four seconds in, four seconds out), and to identify the emotion you are experiencing. As you are doing this, the wave might continue to climb, and that's okay, you're not doing anything wrong. Simply continue to breathe, identify the emotion (don't think about why you are feeling this way) and keep your thoughts on identifying the emotion, and allow it to eventually fade away. Sometimes saying to yourself "I am feeling _____" with each breath can be helpful.

You don't want to analyze why you are feeling this way, or be upset that you are feeling this way. Just keep your thoughts on the emotion.

85. Google "celebrities with anxiety." Some of your favorite people experience a similar fate. Dealing with such an adverse disorder actually breeds creativity as a coping mechanism. This is why so many artists, actors, comedians, and musicians struggle with anxiety. In many cases, if not for their ability to channel their anxiety, they never would have achieved so much.

86. Get creative. Channel your nervous energy into an outlet such as painting, writing, sculpting, acting, music, design, dance, or film production.

87. See a therapist for guidance. Trust us on this one. It's not healthy to let anxiety run unfettered. It's vital to discuss your feelings with someone else, particularly a professional. You'll gain a valuable outside perspective and learn ideas for solving problems you're facing. Therapists are trained, objective listeners who will provide the techniques and resources to relieve your anxiety. Need help finding one? We like this link for ease of use: www.psychologytoday.com/us/therapists.

88. Go to the gym, or join a spin or yoga class. Again, it may take some self-motivation, so dig deep and go!

89. Play a video game—even if you're not a gamer.

90. Take a B-complex vitamin. These nutrients are depleted first when you're anxious or stressed.

91. Eat healthfully! This includes reducing consumption of caffeine, sugar, and processed foods. Caffeine jacks up your nervous system and can cause heart palpitations. Worse, caffeine can trigger panic or anxiety attacks, especially if you have an anxiety disorder. Sugar has similar negative effects in that it acts as an adrenal stimulant and can also cause anxiety or panic attacks.

92. Learn a new sport, like field hockey, lacrosse, kiteboarding, etc. Ask a friend or research it online.

CHAPTER 12

MENTAL FILTERS

The free man is he who does not fear to go to the end of his thought.

—Léon Blum

MY LYING MIND

A "mental filter" sounds sort of cool—like a strainer that filters the bad juju from your brain. Kind of like how an oil filter in a car works to remove the free-floating junk in the oil. Unfortunately, that's not how it works. In this chapter, Dr. McDonagh and I describe how mental filters distort reality into something else. They are a cognitive distortion, or a faulty thought pattern, that can lead to higher levels of anxiety. As a cognitive distortion, mental filters are simply ways that our minds convince us of something that isn't true. These inaccurate thoughts reinforce negative thinking or emotions—like anxiety. Essentially, they take information we receive and discombobulate it into something negative and potentially harmful—sort of like when you order a perfectly delicious pizza and then add anchovies.

What you really need to know about mental filters is this: They are thoughts that cause you to falsely perceive reality.

You receive information in the typical manner, but then route the data through a funky invisible "filter" in your head that you didn't know you had. Think of the mental filter as a pair of sunglasses that skew what enters your mind. This, in turn, negatively impacts your perception of the information received.

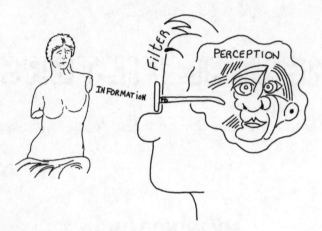

Throughout my teen years, mental filtering was almost a hobby. I negatively filtered everything, never realizing that my perception was not reality. Anxiety and negativity just seemed the norm. Countering mental filters remains a facet of my life to keep anxiety in check. I cannot overemphasize the importance of simply identifying when you are using a mental filter within a particular situation. Recognizing it can prevent a glut of negative outcomes. Sadly, I have lost jobs and relationships from not knowing I was using a mental filter and completely misreading a scenario. But you don't need to suffer the same fate.

Whenever I use mental filters, I literally extract the negative details of a given scenario and amplify them, while filtering out all positive aspects of the incident. Consider a mental filtering example from my recent past. Historically, whenever my dad's name showed as the caller on my cell phone, I would proceed with the following catastrophizing mental filtering process:

"Dad is calling me ..."

Mental Filter (Catastrophizing): OMG! He's going to tell me something terrible has happened! Did something awful happen to Mom?!

Perception: If dad calls, it's definitely to tell me that something terrible has happened to my mother.

Using mental filters, it was not possible that my dad might be calling to share good news; like that he and Mom got a new Hawaiian timeshare where I'd finally get a natural tan. Dad's calls freaked me out. Despite remaining pale in complexion, my dad's calls have never resulted in my catastrophized fears.

An easy way to see your thought process in relation to mental filtering is to use the following simple equation: A + B = C where ...

A: Activating event

B: Belief (this is where mental filters are used)

C: Consequence or your perception from the situation

Put into play, the equation might look something like this:

A: Someone cuts in front of you in line.

B: This guy is a jerk! People should not cut in line, and ought to be more courteous! (Mental filters being used here: Shoulding and Labeling)

C: You become impatient and quite angry.

In reality, there are a few reasons why someone might cut in line somewhere—the primary one being that they simply didn't realize where the end of the line actually was. I've done this numerous times myself, as have most of us. And, remember: Your thoughts don't equal facts. Not all of us consistently pay attention to our surroundings. Many people walk around in a completely oblivious state, falling into potholes and tripping over flat carpet.

What we think determines what happens to us, so if we want to change our lives, we need to stretch our minds.
—Wayne Dyer, self-improvement author and speaker

---

12 MENTAL FILTER TYPES

As mental filters go, there is a wide assortment of types. You'll notice that some of them work similarly to others. Let's review the types you are most likely to use. Keep in mind that this isn't an exhaustive list of all mental filters, rather the most commonly utilized:

1. All-or-Nothing Thinking: In all-or-nothing thinking (aka black-and-white thinking), things are either black or white. There are no gradations, middle ground, or potential options. When thinking with this mental filter, a person splits their views into extremes, leaving little opportunity for alternative views or solutions to a problem. Thinking this way often involves using absolute terms, such as never or every. People who regularly use this filter often believe that they are either successful or complete failures in life. When used, it might appear as follows:

"I have to get an 'A' on my chemistry final or I'm an idiot!"

"If s/he doesn't like me back, then I'm an ugly troll."

"If I don't do well on final exams, I'll never get into a decent college and will serve curly fries out a drive-thru window for life."

2. Discounting the positives: Under the influence of this filter, you are certain that most information received is of the negative persuasion. Even if the data is clearly positive, you will decrease the element of positivity. When you slight the positives in your life, you discount personal successes as mere luck or coincidence and ignore positive achievements. You are unable to recognize how your hard work contributed to the success. When used in real life, it could look like this:

"I got an 'A' on my physics final, but it was because of luck and the curve."

"I scored the winning free throw at last night's basketball game, but it was pure chance."

"Alexis said 'yes' to the dance, but it was likely out of pity for me."

3. Future-tripping: As you learned, this distortion involves looking at a situation and stressing about how it will be a worst-case scenario in the future. It's sort of like whipping out a crystal ball and predicting doom for yourself. It's also a side effect of not remaining in the present moment. Using this filter causes you to worry about the future so much that it's impossible to enjoy the present. Sound at all familiar? In truth, an outstanding outcome is just as likely, and probably more so! Future-tripping might go down like this:

"We're out of milk for cereal, and now the whole day will likely suck."

"I'm hitting every red light on the way to school, which is probably a sign of worse things to come—maybe even an asteroid strike."

"I didn't get the lead role in the school play, and I'll never get an acting gig again, not even on MTV's Teen Mom."

4. Overgeneralization: Another fallacy and thinking error, overgeneralization is when you deduce that because something bad or undesirable happened once, bad things will surely continue as the norm. Rather than seeing a single negative instance as a one-off, you think, since it occurred that way last time, it will continue to go badly. Today may have been a long, tiring, boring day, but that doesn't mean all days are long, tiring, and boring. Life may be difficult at times, but it is also quite fulfilling. Consider the following examples:

"My bestie was too busy to hang with me after practice. She'll always be too busy for me."

"I choked at the recital today. I'll never be able to perform in front of a group."

"A few of the cheerleaders shunned me at the post-game party, so the entire cheerleading squad is pretty much a gaggle of #@!%es!."*

5. Catastrophizing: You'll recall that catastrophizing is a common irrational thought where we believe that something is far worse than it is. It contains an element of future-tripping with gross overgeneralization where you expect the worst to happen, no matter what. It's an assumption of failure before you even start. Three aspects of catastrophizing intensify the filter: Ruminating over a situation, magnifying it greatly, and feeling a sense of powerlessness to do anything about it. Sadly, it can affect your entire outlook in life and create a self-fulfilling prophecy of failure, disappointment, and underachievement. Consider the following examples:

Sarah wanted to attend the concert with friends, but was certain she'd have an anxiety attack from being stuck in the huge crowd and everyone would see. Her night would be ruined, and she would wake up a friendless, emotional "freak."

"I slept through my alarm and I'll be two hours late for work! I'll get fired, have no money, and lose my car, my friends will abandon me over my carelessness, and I'll be overwhelmed by loneliness until it actually kills me!"

6. Jumping to conclusions: A form of catastrophizing, this filter entails predicting a worst-case outcome in the absence of any facts or real information. It is negatively anticipating in a vacuum, as if you knew what others are feeling and why they act the way they do. There are two forms of this cognitive distortion: 1) mind reading and 2) fortune telling. Mind reading assumes that others are adversely assessing you or have bad intentions toward you. Fortune telling is predicting a negative future result or assuming a situation will turn out badly. They might take the following forms:

"My friends are avoiding me because I came out as gay."

"The family of my ex has been against me since she broke up with me."

Cameron was ashamed because several coworkers witnessed his panic attack in the restaurant kitchen. He was certain they already thought less of him for showing signs of anxiety, and now believed they would think he was totally mental. He also worried about losing his job if his managers found out. Cameron concluded that if he lost his job due to anxiety, then no one would hire him again, not even Chipotle in the mall food court.

7. Personalization: Personalizing is a thought distortion where you believe that everything others do or say is a form of direct, personal reaction to you. The result is that you see yourself as the cause of some negative external event for which you were not primarily responsible. People with this thought disorder take things personally by thinking that everything other people think, do, or say is related to them in some way. Consider the following:

"I haven't heard from my boyfriend/girlfriend today. I think s/he's mad at me!"

"My team was unfairly disqualified in only the second round of the debate. I'm certain it was because of an argument I had the week prior with the officiating judge because he hates me."

"The coach always singles me out for extra laps."

8. Fairness fallacy: Using this mental filter leads to feelings of resentment because we think we know what is fair, but the world doesn't necessarily agree with us. We fall prey to this filter by refusing to accept the premise that life isn't always fair. The filter holds an expectation that things should always work out in our favor. However, that's not reality, and expectations often lead to disappointments and resentments. Fortunately, most people work toward fairness. But demanding—or even expecting—equality in all situations is unrealistic and irrational. Holding onto this expectation can do more harm than good.

"I don't feel badly for cheating on my girlfriend, since she cheated on me first."

"My little sister gets to use the car all day on Saturday, and I only get it for a few hours on Friday after school. She doesn't even wash it or fill it with gas! She always gets preferential treatment."

"I'm always picked last for dodgeball because of my puny throwing arm."

9. Blaming: When using this filter, you blame others and hold them responsible for your problems or pain, taking your attention off the actual problem. It includes a side dish of refusal-to-accept-responsibility for undesirable events. And, why not? It's much easier to blame others than to take responsibility for negative outcomes, or to simply blame whenever you feel badly. The blaming filter may take one of the following forms:

"I only yelled profanities at my mom because she purposely ruined my concert plans by assigning lame chores. It's her fault she made me so mad."

"I wouldn't have posted that humiliating picture of her if she wasn't so rude to me at school."

"He made me feel stupid in front of everyone."

10. Shoulding: As mental filters go, this one is my favorite because I should myself often. We all maintain an internal list of rules about how others should behave, and it makes us angry when people break them. When using this mental filter, your automatic thought is that you or someone else should/must/ought to/has to do something that aligns with your internal belief schema. When you direct should statements toward others who go against your demands, you end up feeling only anger and frustration. We cannot dictate the agenda of others based on our whims and beliefs. And should statements directed at ourselves typically lead to guilt, when there are often sound reasons why you don't do what you should/ought to do at any given time. Shoulding might appear as such:

"I really should exercise more and not be such a sloth."

"He shouldn't interrupt me when I'm talking."

"People must not drive so selfishly."

"I should be doing my homework right now, but I'd rather TikTok."

"I should stop eating so much stuffed-crust pizza."

11. Emotional reasoning: When using emotional reasoning, you believe that what you feel must be true regardless of any evidence. If you feel stupid or unattractive, then it must be factual. You simply accept that your unhealthy feelings accurately reflect the way things really are. With this mental filter, thoughts and feelings do equal facts, and you actually fight to prove that your opinions are right. And, why not, since you are accepting your emotions as evidence of truth! When using this cognitive distortion, you aren't likely to challenge the validity of your perception that's making you feel so anxious and depressed. It can take the following forms:

"Since I'm feeling jealous, it must mean that my boyfriend/ girlfriend is cheating on me."

"I feel overwhelmed and hopeless; therefore, my problems must be impossible to solve."

"I feel inadequate, so I must be a worthless person."

"I'm not in the mood to do anything, so I might as well stay in bed and listen to some EDM combos."

12. Labeling: Labeling is an extreme form of overgeneralizing. When you label as a mental filter, you generalize one or two qualities into a negative universal judgment about yourself or another person. Making a single broad assumption about someone based on one to a few isolated traits is almost always incorrect. Labeling can appear as follows:

You label your sister's boyfriend as a "loser" while not being open to any proof that he's not actually a loser.

"I'm such an idiot for failing my driver's test today!"

"That guy is a selfish jerk for being rude to the server."

Because she's often late to work, she must be irresponsible.

You label someone as stuck up, when they're actually just extremely shy.

You call yourself a "whale" because you look fat in the mirror.

Men are disturbed not by things, but by the view which they take of them.

—Epictetus

I have the uncanny ability to use multiple filters at once to my own anxious peril. I've even been known to combine filters for concurrent usage as super-hybrid filters that spin me into record-setting, frenzied vortices of anxiety. Take my dating life, for example. In the past, when meeting a girl I really liked, it was not unlike me to engage all of the most common cognitive distortions at once in an impressive, but calamitous array of cerebral dysfunction. It would go play out something like this:

Alicia is the single best girl I've ever met. She's the epitome of hot. I have to make her mine, or I'll be devastated (all-or-nothing, with a pinch of catastrophizing). She shows considerable interest in me when we're together, but clearly it's not because I'm attractive or worthy (discounting the positives). This will never work, though. She's too good for me and way outta my league. Things might go along for a while, but she will eventually blow me off without warning and rip my heart out like an Aztec warrior princess (future-tripping). Sara dumped me last year, so obviously, this potential relationship won't work either (overgeneralization). If Alicia decides to stop seeing me, my world will plummet into a cataclysmic spiral of doom, culminating in a terminal state of depression and self-loathing. I will be relegated to the annals of dating history, and marked "unworthy" by girls school district-wide. I'm kinda certain she's already plotting her exit strategy (catastrophizing with a healthy dose of jumping to conclusions). I bet her friends are telling her that she's too good for me. I mean, I know she has always been the "dumper," leaving a trail of broken guys in her past (overgeneralizing again). Maybe not a trail, but I know she left her last boyfriend. Clearly she's a maniacal heartbreaker lacking remorse or the ability to feel pain (labeling).

Fast forward three months …

I can't believe she dumped me! I knew she was a soulless tormentor! (Labeling with a fistful of overgeneralization.) It's totally my fault. I cared too much. I was "the nice guy" and too attentive to her. I made her leave me (personalization). I'm sure her friends had a lot to do with this! They never thought I was cool enough to be with her because I'm a writer for the school paper, and not a jock. I thought "the pen was mightier than the sword"—or football. Doesn't anyone appreciate neurotic journalists anymore?! (Jumping to conclusions, overgeneralization, and labeling, with a special guest appearance by blaming). It must be true—I wasn't good enough for her. She left me, proving I'm a two-time loser (emotional reasoning). I swear, nothing good ever works out for me! Life is so unfair (fairness fallacy). Sure, I won $500 in fantasy football, but that was just chance. I should've played it cooler with her. I must've scared her away with how much I cared. I should've just backed off a bit and acted like I didn't care (shoulding). All girls are crazy! (Labeling.) Whoa … hold up … is Janelle the head cheerleader checking me out right now?!

A mental filter in use looks like this:

DR. TOM'S TAKE

MENTAL FILTERING, A BUCKET FOR ANXIOUS THOUGHTS

Recognizing mental filters is a great way to start exercising control over your anxious thoughts. There are two benefits to recognizing our mental filters, and both are discussed below. Jon covered several common types of thinking errors related to anxiety. Think of mental filters as a category or a bucket for you to place your thoughts. When you start looking at all of your anxious thoughts, you will recognize a pattern. Most of us have thoughts that fall within all of these mental filters at one point or another, but if you look at your anxious thoughts closely, there's a good chance you can identify two or three that are more common for you.

BENEFITS TO CATEGORIZING THOUGHTS INTO MENTAL FILTERS

This first benefit to labeling thoughts is that it helps to create a sense of separation from you and your anxious thinking. This will give you more control in the moment. The more control we recognize we have over our thoughts, the less anxious we will feel. Very often anxiety continues because we feel like we don't have any say in what happens in our minds. We feel like the anxiety takes over and is running the show. By creating this separation from our thoughts (almost like you are observing the thoughts from above), we get back into the driver's seat and remember that we are bigger than our anxiety.

The principle of life is that life responds by corresponding; your life becomes the thing you have decided it shall be.
—Raymond Charles Barker, founder and first minister of The Church of Religious Science

---

In addition to creating separation from our thoughts, the second benefit is the value of recognizing that the thoughts themselves aren't totally true. Our anxiety tends to distort or skew how we see, think, and feel things that make us feel anxious. Imagine if you put on a pair of red-tinted sunglasses. Everything you see would be a shade of red. The same thing happens with anxiety and our thoughts. Everything that happens to you gets filtered through these anxiety sunglasses, making your thoughts more anxious than what the situation calls for. It's not fair. It's like getting blamed for something you didn't do … all the time. Thankfully, it doesn't have to be like this. There is a way to take these shades off. And the way to do that is simply learning about the mental filters for anxiety.

Find Your Filters

Review the 12 common anxiety mental filters discussed above. While you might be able to say that your anxious thoughts fit into all 12, try to pick out the top two or three that apply the most to you. Most people have a sort of "greatest hits" list of mental filters that happen to them time and time again.

Write your top two or three mental filters.

1. _____

2. _____

3. _____

Now, write down a thought that corresponds to each filter.

1. _____

_____

2. _____

_____

3. _____

_____

After you have written down the corresponding thoughts, try to challenge them and see why they aren't true. Here are some examples:

Mental filter: Future-tripping

Thought: I got a bad grade. I'm going to flunk out of school and never get into college.

Challenge: Yes, I got a bad grade and I don't like it, but one low score does not determine the rest of my life.

Mental filter: Mind-reading

Thought: Everybody is judging me right now.

Challenge: Some people do judge, but it's probably not everyone in the room. It's more likely other people are focused with how they appear than judging how I look.

Write challenges to your thoughts.

1. _____

2. _____

3. _____

At some point each day, get into the habit of writing/typing the mental filter, thought, and challenge when you are feeling anxious. At the end of the day works, but the closer you can do this to when you feel anxious, the better. By doing it over and over again, you will actually change how you think in anxious moments. The more you write/type this out, the faster your brain will start thinking correctly on its own. However, don't expect this change to happen suddenly. Your brain has regularly been using these mental filters for a long time. So it makes sense that it would take some time for it to adjust to a new way of thinking. Be patient and keep at it.

> *Build up your weaknesses until they become your strong points.*
>
> —Knute Rockne, renowned University of Notre Dame football player and coach

ACTIVITY
Identify the Challenge

Fill in the challenge sections:

Mental filter: Shoulding

Thought: I shouldn't be feeling like this right now.

Challenge: _____

Mental filter: Emotional reasoning

Thought: I feel so stupid. I am stupid.

Challenge: _____

Mental filter: Catastrophizing

Thought: No! I can't handle this! It's the worst thing ever! I will die!

Challenge: _____

Mental filter: Personalization

Thought: My boyfriend/girlfriend left me, and it's all my fault.

Challenge: _____

_____

WAYS TO ALLEVIATE ANXIETY

93. Pick a goal, and go after it. There is likely at least one productivity or personal interest goal that you've had planned but have thus far avoided. Whatever you decide to pursue, work toward it little by little each day. Living without purpose or meaning will greatly contribute to anxiety and/or depression. The key is to pick attainable goals that are workable.

94. Teach yourself to snap a bottle cap.

95. Shuffle a deck of cards over and over (it's soothing).

96. Start positive self-talk to counter negative chatter ("I feel terrible now, but I will overcome this!").

97. Schedule your worry time and postpone all worry until that 30-minute assigned time. It's non-negotiable.

98. Find a self-defense/martial arts/MMA class and do a free trial.

99. Do as many freestanding body squats as you're able.

CHAPTER 13

ANXIETY AND SLEEP

The only time I have problems is when I sleep.

—Tupac Shakur

SILENT LUCIDITY

Teenagers today don't get enough sleep, so Dr. McDonagh and I wrote a chapter to help you get more ZZZs. I love to sleep, but my mind hates letting me. The mere act of lying down to doze indicates that it's time to ponder all my current worries and anxieties. These thoughts are typically stresses carried over from the day and can include any of the following:

Did I lock the front door? I wonder why my workout sucked today. I need to pick up my dry cleaning. Did I leave any of my pets outside? I don't have bananas for my breakfast smoothie. Or yogurt. OMG, it's 12:27 and I'm still awake! I'm going to be so tired tomorrow. I hope we don't have that overdue mega-quake tonight. Where is my earthquake survival pack? I forgot to call Grandma. Why

*does my knee always itch in the exact same spot? I think I left
the kitchen window open. What if a prowler sneaks in and clubs
me unconscious? Will I sleep then? I'm hungry. Didn't I just eat?
Maybe I'm thirsty. Did I brush my teeth? Is that my car alarm
going off? When was the last time I had any vegetables? I hope I
don't get sick from that woman coughing in line at Target. I wonder
what she had. Was it communicable? Why did I spend $29 on
salmon-flavored cat toothpaste? OMG, it's 1:19 and I'm still awake!
I'm going to be so tired tomorrow. I have to fall asleep. I have to try
harder. Must ... fall ... asleep. What if I never fell asleep again?
How long would it take to die from sleeplessness? Did I leave my
card in the ATM earlier? Maybe I should read for a while. If I fall
asleep right now I can still get five hours of rest. I love this book.
Why don't I read more? I better check my weather app so I know
what to wear tomorrow. Oh look, I have 58 new emails ...*

---

*If a man had as many ideas during the day as he does when he
has insomnia, he'd make a fortune.*

—Griff Niblack, author

The irony of losing sleep over anxieties is that it renders you useless
to resolve your concerns the next day because you'll be too tired. Few
things are actually worth losing sleep over, and being tired never
helped anyone to conquer anything. In my case, I would stay up late
reading until I finally passed out at 2 a.m. with the lights on, only to
awaken to the alarm a few hours later, which I would snooze every
nine minutes for an hour until I finally got up just to drag all day long.
I let my poor sleep habits reign until I was 16 and working as a city
government driver. I would drive all around town taking important
municipal documents here and there, until one afternoon the hypnotic
drone of wheels on pavement lulled me to sleep as I merged onto the
freeway. Fortunately, I dozed off toward the right shoulder unknowingly steering the white car marked "For Official Business" into a long
row of tall and forgiving drought-tolerant ornamental shrubs.

The injured branches and debris beating past the windows sounded like a hulking tree monster slashing the car apart with talons of sinewy bark. Even the exhaust system was ripped from underneath before the car halted atop a woody shrub, smoke wisping from both sides. My heart hammered as I tumbled out the door to study the damage. Branches and limbs jutted from everywhere. But I was alive and the engine was still running. I tore the branches from their strangleholds, jumped back into the disgraced car, and drove to my dad's house with the residual kindling and exhaust pipes following behind in a trail of sparks. Having a dad with a welder and the skills of MacGyver saved the car—and my job. But he couldn't save me from my sleepy self; that would take more than a welding torch.

TODAY'S SLEEP-DEPRIVED TEENS

The feeling of sleepiness when you are not in bed and can't get there is the meanest feeling in the world.
—Edgar Watson Howe, novelist and essayist

According to studies, today's teens are more sleep deprived than ever. Reasons for the trend are uncertain, but a Columbia University public health researcher, Katherine Keyes, said factors that might have contributed include increasing use of social media, smart phones, and other electronics, and rising rates of obesity, which has been linked with sleep deprivation. According to an exhaustive 2015 study by Common Sense Media, teenagers spend nearly nine hours a day immersed in electronic media. Other research suggests that early school start times play a role, and advocates have been pushing for later times for teens.

According to the National Sleep Foundation (NSF), teens need 8 to 10 hours of sleep per night to function at their best. Researchers who analyzed the University of Michigan's annual Monitoring the Future national surveys of youth behavior, found that "more than half of kids aged 15 and older would need to sleep at least two hours more each night to meet recommendations for adequate rest, increasing concerns about the impact on their health and academic performance." A lack of sleep can result in dire consequences, such as:

o An inability to learn, focus, and cognitively function.
o Being more prone to acne and poor skin.
o Irritability leading to hostile or inappropriate behavior.
o Increased caffeine and even nicotine use.
o Lowered immunity resulting in illness.
o Fatigue and susceptibility to injury.
o Reduction in driver reaction times equal to levels as severe as driving drunk.
o Poor decision-making ability.
o Loss in overall productivity.
o Decrease in overall competency and intellect.

There is a direct correlation between a lack of sleep and anxiety/ depression. Stress and anxiety may cause sleeping problems or make existing problems worse. And having an anxiety disorder exacerbates the problem. But which comes first, the anxiety or the insomnia? Either. Anxiety causes sleeping problems, and new research suggests sleep deprivation can cause an anxiety disorder. Research also shows that some form of sleep disruption is present in nearly all psychiatric disorders. Studies also show that people with chronic insomnia are at high risk of developing an anxiety disorder.

Kids today have incredibly demanding schedules with school, jobs, sports, and extracurricular activities, and they are simply not assigning enough value to sleep. The effects of chronic sleep loss are even more disconcerting and can include scary stuff like heart disease, heart attack, heart failure, irregular heartbeat, high blood pressure, stroke, and diabetes. In other words, sleep—whether temporary or permanent—always wins in the end.

Nothing cures insomnia like the realization that it's time to get up.

GO-TO-SLEEP TECHNIQUE

Like many teens, I didn't take the sleep notion seriously and was on and off sleep meds for much of my teen years. In time and with some work, I was able to conquer my sleep woes.

First, I weaned off the medication and began a regular sleep schedule. I stopped the afternoon caramel macchiatos and reading dimmed electronics in bed. I disallowed any worrying at night. Instead, I scheduled official worry time for a 30-minute period—no more, no less—in the mornings. This remains nonnegotiable. But nothing helped as much as one principal technique I've used every night since my teens. It's a modest meditative skill that helps me to fall asleep fast. It was challenging at first, like I was doing pull-ups with my brain. But I kept at it. It will change your world. Here's how:

1. Once you are settled into bed, take notice of your breath. Mentally follow your gentle inhalations and exhalations while focusing on how the air feels as it passes through your nostrils. Make the sensation of your breathing your home base.

2. Even as you focus on your breath, you may notice thoughts crossing your mindscape. Don't mentally cling to any of them; just take note as they pass through your mind without giving them attention. Depending upon how anxious you feel, they may be coming in a flurry or a trickle.

3. Keep your focus on your breath, your presence and stillness. Practice not thinking. Even as thoughts will surely arise, wanting your attention, then subside.

4. Maintain this stillness for as long as possible, while recentering yourself away from any passing thoughts and back to your breath. Soon you will fall asleep.

5. If you awaken, relax and repeat.

This is an example of managing anxiety symptoms with a cognitive skill that mitigates anxious thoughts, rather than taking a pill.

DR. TOM'S TAKE

SLEEP: WHY IT'S ELUSIVE AND HOW TO GET IT

Much like the chicken or the egg question, it can be difficult at times to determine if sleep problems are creating anxiety, or if anxiety is creating sleep problems. In either case, it's good to know that if you are able to work on promoting good sleep habits and increasing the quality of your sleep, your anxiety symptoms will likely benefit as well. Jon's Go-to-Sleep Technique is a good start. Here are more approaches to counteract anxious sleep thoughts.

THOUGHTS

The theme of our thoughts when we are having difficulty falling asleep is the same as other anxiety symptoms: "Danger! Worst-Case Scenarios and Catastrophizing!" We create these absolute truths (aka thinking errors) in our minds automatically without realizing we're doing it. It happens because that's the way our brains work. So try not to blame yourself!

With anxious sleep thoughts, the general lie we tell ourselves is something like "Receiving a magic number of sleep hours will keep the worst-case scenario from happening." Like most anxious thoughts, these beliefs aren't the easiest things to recognize right away. You probably have to do some mental digging to find them. They're not unconscious, but just beneath the surface of your awareness.

Some of the time, these worst-case scenarios have to do with your health, like, "If I don't sleep I'm going to die!" But, mostly, they are focused on your ability to function the next day. "I won't be able to focus in school, and I'm not going to remember anything for the test!" We create these rules in our heads and convince ourselves that unless things happen the exact way we would like them to happen, chaos will ensue.

During these times, your job is to remember that just because you think it does not make it true. Thoughts and feelings do not equal facts. Don't believe everything you think! And, torture tactics aside, you can't die from a lack of sleep. Your body will grab moments of microsleep automatically. This is why it's a bad time to drive when you're feeling fatigued. Your concentration levels can also become more impaired, and you will feel more irritable and less tolerant of daily annoyances. But that's really about it. The worst-case scenario isn't possible.

Just so you know, Randy Gardner holds the Guinness World Record for staying awake for the longest period of time: 11 days and 24 minutes. He was monitored by medical professionals the entire time. The experiment concluded that long-term sleep deprivation has limited medical problems aside from mood issues. So, unless you plan on staying awake for over 11 days, science says you'll be okay. At least temporarily.

BEHAVIORS

When addressing sleep issues, it can be helpful to think of your mind and body as an advanced tool that works on reinforcement. So when it comes to sleep difficulties, part of the solution has to include a focus on what your mind and body are being reinforced to do. If you are having problems with sleep, chances are your behaviors are inadvertently reinforcing your sleep problems.

With this in mind, let's concentrate on behavioral actions you can take. There are two actions to consider. The first addresses effective sleep behavioral reinforcement techniques; the second addresses good sleep habits.

1. ASSOCIATING YOUR BED WITH SLEEP

If you are having problems with sleep, chances are you are staying awake in bed, tossing and turning while trying to convince yourself to fall asleep. This is the approach most people take because eventually they will fall asleep, even if only for a short time. But there is a problem with this method.

If you keep in mind the idea that your mind and body are a tool, by staying awake in bed for a significant period of time, you are training yourself to stay awake! Your unconscious mind and body don't know any better. They go for the most reinforced behavior, not the most helpful behavior. So, at a deeper thinking level, your brain is starting to believe your bed is a place to be awake. This is something that you want to stop, and you can do so with relative ease through simple adjustments. If your brain can be reinforced to respond in one way (being awake in bed), it can be reinforced to respond in a different way (being asleep in bed). Our brains just work like that. It's called malleability.

So, how do you make this adjustment? If you find that you are having difficulty falling asleep and it has been about 20 minutes (there are varying opinions on the time frame, ranging from 10 to 30 minutes), get out of bed. If you can, go into another room. If you can't, try sitting on the floor or in another area of your room. Getting out of bed does not mean you are throwing in the towel for that night's sleep, it means you are trying to retrain yourself. You want the deeper level of thinking in your brain to think the bed is for sleep only.

When you are out of bed, the goal is to do activities that promote sleep. So, things that are activating (video games, looking at your phone/computer/tablet, drinking soda, etc.) are out. Some helpful things include reading, listening to music or podcasts, doing relaxation and breathing exercises, or writing down things you have to do the next day so you don't forget them and don't feel the need to mentally hold on to them through the night. There are many different things you can do, but the most important is to avoid those that increase your energy and make you more active.

Only go back to bed when you start to feel tired and are ready to fall asleep. Maintaining this routine will help to retrain your mind that the bed is for sleep only. If you have been up for several hours, chances are you are not engaging in an activity that is relaxing or promotes sleep. Remember, your body has a natural drive to sleep. You engage this natural drive for sleep by following through with this plan.

2. SLEEP HYGIENE

You can also promote the body's natural drive to sleep by engaging in good sleep habits before you go to bed with a regular pre-bedtime routine. This routine should start about 30 minutes before you want to fall asleep and include putting the electronics down (the light makes your brain think the sun is still up), brushing your teeth, and other normal wind-down daily activities.

The National Sleep Foundation also recommends the following: No naps, avoid caffeine (at least after 3 p.m.), exercise in the morning or afternoon (avoid late night exercise as it can increase your body temperature, making it harder to sleep), avoid large meals right before bedtime, and make your sleep environment as comfortable as possible.

Not being able to sleep is terrible. You have the misery of having partied all night—without the satisfaction.

—Lynn Johnston, cartoonist

WHEN TO SEE A PROFESSIONAL

If you have tried the above recommendations for at least a few weeks and haven't found them helpful, it might be time to see a professional. It's possible there could be a medical issue, so be sure to talk to your general practitioner. If your doctor rules out any medical issues, there are very effective treatments mental health professionals use to help people with sleep problems. Try to see someone who specializes in sleep or has had training in cognitive behavioral therapy for insomnia (CBT-I). This is a well-researched, evidence-based approach that is very effective at helping people who have sleep problems. And they work for Jon!

WAYS TO ALLEVIATE ANXIETY

100. Download a soothing meditative sound app—especially to use at bedtime.

101. Floss your teeth.

102. Put your phone in a different room, a drawer, closet, car trunk, etc. See how long you can entertain yourself without looking at it.

103. Using a pencil, try to shade a piece of paper evenly, going from very dark to very light.

104. List as many cities in the US that you can. Don't stop until the only things you can think of are cities.

105. Take a fish oil supplement. Studies continue to show that taking a fish oil supplement containing both the potent omega-3 fatty acids, EPA and DHA, can help with symptoms of depression, anxiety, and even bipolar disorder.

106. Memorize a Bible/Koran/Torah/scripture verse or the lyrics to a favorite song.

Chapter 14

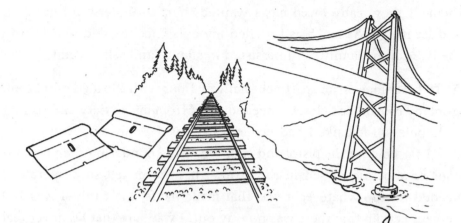

SELF-HARM AND SUICIDE

The brain is an organ. Mental illnesses are illnesses of that organ. Brain scans show that there is a physical difference between a healthy brain and a sick brain. Telling someone "You're not really sick. It's all in your head" is like telling someone with asthma "It's not real, it's all in your lungs." The brain is an organ that can malfunction as much as any other organ.

—Unknown

GETTING CANDID ABOUT SUICIDE

This chapter isn't just statistics and adult-speak to cheer you up. It's heavy, visceral, and an essential part of any topic that includes anxiety or depression. Dr. McDonagh and I need to get straight and vulnerable with you because you deserve that from us. On a personal note, I hope that by now you know I've not only traveled a similar journey as you, but I still work at it today. I spent part of my teen years in a hopeless, dark cycle of despair. I was incredibly angry at people for loving me because it meant I couldn't go through with killing myself and hurting them. If they really loved me, I wanted them to understand my pain and let me go. As much as I reviled my existence, I could not destroy the lives of my family. So, I persisted in silence and self-loathing.

At 18 I sat alone on an apartment hallway floor with a loaded gun I took from my roommate's closet. I needed relief from my anxiety and feeling so hopeless. I felt like I had never really lived—only survived day to day. I sat holding the pistol and sobbing while pondering the pros and cons of shooting myself in the head. I had never felt so desperate. I needed to stop whatever it was that made me feel so badly. I was 100 percent certain that there was no way out. I was sure that I'd never feel anything other than despondency. But I was 100 percent wrong. No matter how badly you feel in any given moment, it gets better. As I sat crying with the gun in my lap, I performed an internal debate that went something like this:

Jon's Suicide Pros:

1. I will permanently end my pain.
2. ... uh
3. ...

Jon's Suicide Cons:

1. I will transfer the pain to those who loved me.
2. I will become a fading memory over time.
3. I will never realize or fulfill my life's purpose.
4. The last thing people will see of me are the contents of my head splattered everywhere.
5. I might survive my attempt, suffering in a vegetative state with half a brain.
6. I will ruin the lives of my family, which is far worse than just my suffering.

7. What are the spiritual repercussions? Will I face an angry God for what I had done?

It was numbers 6 and 7 above that stopped me from ever taking that final step. I pulled myself back together and made a call for help. I spent the next few days safe in a hospital in Oakland, California, where I felt so low I could no longer eat or function. I was nourished intravenously for a few days until I could regain some strength. Though I could not take my own life, I was somehow shutting down. If, during that period of depression, you told me that one day I would actually be happy, I would have told you off. But you would have been right. My life was still a promise unfulfilled, as is yours today. I intensely recall my dad standing by my bedside asking me to find the will to press on. Seeing the hurt in his eyes gave me enough reason to fight for him, if not for myself. I was eventually released from the hospital, but my fight was far from over. I continued self-harm with substance abuse for many years thereafter, until I began to accept who I was and became a proponent for "me"—to the point of actually loving myself. Something that had formerly seemed impossible.

Life is amazing. And then it's awful. And it's amazing again. And in between the amazing and awful it's ordinary and mundane and routine. Breathe in the amazing, hold on through the awful, and relax and exhale during the ordinary. That's just living heartbreaking, soul-healing, amazing, awful, ordinary life. And it's breathtakingly beautiful.

—L. R. Knost, best-selling parenting and children's book author

---

Taking things day to day made a huge difference. So much changes in a 24-hour period, including your state of mind. And here's the kicker: It takes far more strength and resolve to live than to die. This is reflected in a distressing statistic: Teen suicide is the third-leading cause of death for young people ages 15 to 24. And, according to the American Psychological Association (APA), mental illness—including anxiety—is the leading risk factor for suicide. One in five teenagers in the US seriously considers suicide annually, according to data collected by the CDC. But most people who consider suicide don't really want to die; they just don't know how to cope with or alleviate the pain they are experiencing. Later in this chapter, Dr. McDonagh will discuss why suicidal thoughts emerge and how to prevent self-harm.

You are here for a reason. It will unfold for you in time. And if you're alive, you have the opportunity to do whatever you want in this world. You have plenty of time to figure out your reason for being. Life will give you a lot to bear. Your promise and purpose are concealed in there somewhere.

A LESSON FROM VIKTOR FRANKL

One of the most poignant examples of suffering and loss is the story of Viktor Frankl, a physician and psychiatrist who survived four Nazi concentration and death camps, including the infamous Auschwitz. Frankl epitomized the words of Nietzsche: "He who has a Why to live for can bear almost any How."

As a prisoner, Frankl kept himself and his hopes alive by a desire to see his wife again and one day teach about man's quest for meaning. Sadly, Frankl's parents, brother, and pregnant wife were killed; but he was able to cope, source the importance of it all, and move forward with a renewed life purpose to include writing one of the most moving and significant books of our time, Man's Search for Meaning. Frankl teaches us that "If there is a meaning in life at all, there must be a meaning in suffering. Suffering is an eradicable part of life, even as fate and death. Without suffering and death human life cannot be complete." We all face the opportunity to achieve something through our own suffering. Our unique opportunity lies in the way we bear our burden, and in our attitude toward difficulty while pondering our meaning. Make no mistake; you have a decisive and purposeful meaning in this world. For many of us, it takes suffering and hardship to find it. It's incredible pressure that puts the shine into a diamond.

Over a four-year period as a psychiatrist, Frankl saw some 12,000 depressed patients, most of them admitted after a suicide attempt. Frankl wrote, "Patients have repeatedly told me how happy they were that the suicide attempt had not been successful; weeks, months, years later, they told me it turned out that there was a solution to their problem, an answer to their question, a meaning to their life. But you have to live to see the day on which it may happen, so you have to survive in order to see that day dawn, and from now on the responsibility for survival does not leave you."

Everything can be taken from a man but one thing: the last of the human freedoms—to choose one's attitude in any given set of circumstances, to choose one's own way.

—Viktor Frankl

GOLDEN GATE BRIDGE SURVIVOR STORIES

The Golden Gate Bridge is the most popular suicide spot in the United States, perhaps even the world. Having been born in San Francisco and adopted from Oakland, California, I spent a fair amount of time with the Golden Gate Bridge within eyesight. Beyond its notable beauty and iconic symbolism is a dark lure for those seeking to end their lives. At the time of this writing, more than 2,100 people have jumped to their deaths from the Golden Gate Bridge, with 21 confirmed suicides in 2021 alone, and four suspected (no bodies were found). Two or three people jump each month as work to finish a permanent suicide barrier shuffles along. Between 100 and 200 more are stopped each year by the bridge patrol and California Highway Patrol officers. Again, there is something remarkable to source from these tragedies:

> Fewer than 35 people have survived a jump from the Golden Gate Bridge. And nearly each one reported that the moment they leapt from the bridge, they regretted their action and wanted to live.

Consider the story of one such survivor, Kevin Hines: "The millisecond my hands left the rail, it was an instant regret," he says. In that moment, he remembers thinking, "No one's gonna know that I didn't want to die."

And then, there is the equally harrowing experience of Ken Baldwin, who knew he'd made a mistake as soon as his arms let go. Ken had walked coolly onto the bridge and jumped over the rail. *Psychology Today* reported, "Despite all his years of contemplating suicide, he knew that he didn't want to die after all. As he describes it, 'I thought, What am I doing? This was the worst thing I could do in my life. I didn't want to die. I wanted to live.' He recalls realizing that 'everything in my life that I'd thought was unfixable was totally fixable—except for having just jumped.'" Once he recovered from his injuries, Ken experienced intense gratitude for life that he exhibits today as a high school teacher. It took nearly losing his life to realize how much he actually valued living. Kevin and Ken personify the universal notion of regret by those who attempt suicide.

Anxiety—which can be experienced as guilt, self-blame, threat of social exclusion, ostracism, and worry—seems to be a common strand in the majority of suicides.

The person who completes suicide dies once. Those left behind die a thousand deaths, trying to relive those terrible moments and understand ... why?

—Unknown

SUICIDE CLUSTERS

Another SF Bay Area city, the affluent town of Palo Alto, received worldwide attention last decade for the number of high school suicides at two campuses: Palo Alto High School ("Paly") and Gunn High School. In the 2009–2010 school year, six students associated with the Palo Alto School District killed themselves. Then, between October 2014 and March 2015, three more students committed suicide. *The Atlantic Monthly* provided some grim figures:

The 10-year suicide rate for the two high schools is between four and five times the national average. Starting in the spring of 2009 and stretching over nine months, three Gunn students, one incoming freshman, and one recent graduate had put themselves in front of an oncoming Caltrain. Another recent graduate had hung himself. While the intervening years had been quieter, they had not been comforting. School counselors remained "overwhelmed and overloaded" with an influx of kids considered high risk, says Roni Gillenson, who has helped oversee Gunn's mental health program since 2006. Twelve percent of Palo Alto high school students surveyed in the 2013–14 school year reported having seriously contemplated suicide in the previous 12 months.

There's nothing sexy, romantic, or nostalgic about death. It's gruesome. It's painful. It will tear your family to shreds. And the last thing you'll feel is regret—but it will be too late.

We know from literature that academic pressure can cause anxiety and depression, which in turn can lead to suicides. Suicide clusters are a group of three or more suicides in close time or geographic proximity. They are rare; on average, five per year occur in the United States, and they are most common among adolescents, college students, prisoners, and soldiers. Suicide clusters thrive on viral news via social connections. NBA star and 2006 graduate of Palo Alto High School Jeremy Lin described via social media how he negotiated the academic and societal pressures as a teen:

As each year of high school passed by, I realized that even though there was pressure to be great, I had to make a personal choice not to define myself by my success and accomplishments. I learned through my brother, my pastor, and my friends that my identity and my worth were in more than my grades. Growing up my parents always said, "Do your best and trust God with the results." When I learned to truly understand what that meant, it was like a weight had been lifted off my shoulders. Separating myself from my results is not an easy lesson and I've had to relearn this in every stage of my life. The world will always need you to accomplish more, do more, and succeed more. After I got into Harvard there was the pressure to get good grades and stand out at Harvard. After "Linsanity" there was the pressure to have great performances every night, to become an All-Star, to win championships. I still dream big and give my all in everything I do, but I know that success and failure are both fleeting.

If you feel you are in a crisis, whether or not you are thinking about killing yourself, please call the National Suicide Prevention Lifeline. Here's a message from the organization:

People have called us for help with substance abuse, economic worries, relationship and family problems, sexual orientation, illness, getting over abuse, depression, mental and physical illness, and even loneliness. When you dial 988, you are calling the crisis center in the Lifeline network closest to your location. After you call, you will hear a message saying you have reached the National Suicide Prevention Lifeline. You will hear hold music while your call is being routed. You will be helped by a skilled, trained crisis worker who will listen to your problems and will tell you about mental health services in your area. Your call is confidential and free. Visit https://988lifeline.org.

NOT THE "EASY WAY OUT"

Some people say that suicide is selfish and "the easy way out." Their reasoning for this is that life is hard for everyone, so those who decide to kill themselves to escape the pain and adversities of life aren't as strong as the rest of us who choose to continue living. But we all process suffering in our way. And no one can rightfully judge what someone else is thinking and feeling. Since he was someone who struggled with this dilemma, I often ponder Robin Williams, a fellow SF Bay Area resident that I've admired since childhood. He gave his life bringing laughter and joy to others. And when he died, it shocked and saddened us. The day after Robin Williams's suicide, the National Suicide Prevention Lifeline fielded the greatest number of calls in its history.

> *All it takes is a beautiful fake smile to hide an injured soul and they will never notice how broken you really are.*
>
> —Robin Williams

Man's most basic instinct is to survive. It is my personal opinion that those who commit suicide are not weak or selfish. Nor did they want to die; but the pain and hopelessness override everything else. This is tragic because of the agonizing wake they leave behind, and the fact that things always shift if given the chance. Life gives us all pain; it also gives us joy. There is no such thing as life without suffering or life void of all joy. We must learn to navigate the good and bad while enjoying the good and knowing that the bad will pass. It always does. As someone with anxiety, you tend to cling to the bad while discounting the good. Even while experiencing goodness, the anxious often struggle to enjoy it because we're waiting for the next bad thing to occur. Remember: 85 percent of the stuff we worry about ends up having a positive or neutral outcome.

Perspective and attitude change everything. Everything.

REACH OUT TO OTHERS

There will be times in life when you feel you are drowning in too much pain with no one to help. But humans were made to synergistically rely upon others. Jodi Picoult captures the idea in her novel *Second Glance*: "Heroes didn't leap tall buildings or stop bullets with an outstretched hand; they didn't wear boots and capes. They bled, and they bruised, and their superpowers were as simple as listening, or loving. Heroes were ordinary people who knew that even if their own lives were impossibly knotted, they could untangle someone else's. And maybe that one act could lead someone to rescue you right back."

We are supposed to feel like we can't handle things alone sometimes. That's when we find the grace of God or community through other people. In times when life becomes unmanageable, we need to be willing to ask for help and support one another. It's by design. We can be with one another in the midst of suffering, helping each other bear the weight. Part of life is the realization that sometimes we can't make it on our own. For some, myself included, a spiritual leader is a person to whom you can turn and say, "I have a burden that I cannot bear." All it takes is walking into a local church, mosque, synagogue, or temple and asking for help.

If you are religious (or even if you are not) and have access to a spiritual leader, try talking to him or her. Like mental health professionals, those in ministry are trained to help people in crisis, particularly those in despair and feeling suicidal.

DR. TOM'S TAKE

"FINE" IS A FOUR-LETTER WORD THAT BEGINS WITH "F"

It's perfectly okay not to feel fine. It's not okay to punish yourself for it. In some cases, people with anxiety will engage in self-harming behaviors and have thoughts or attempts of suicide. If you have anxiety, it does not mean that eventually you will act and feel this way. But it does happen for some people. This section will expand on Jon's advice to include an explanation as to why these thoughts and behaviors emerge. I will also discuss what you can do if you feel like this applies to you.

Live to the point of tears.

—Albert Camus

SELF-HARM/SELF-INJURY

Self-harm is when someone intentionally injures a part of their body, but does not want to kill themselves. For example, cutting (taking a sharp instrument, such as a razor blade, and making cuts on the skin) is a type of self-harming behavior. There are many types of self-harming behaviors. They can include cutting, carving, scratching, pinching, burning, hair pulling, or hitting oneself with an object.

Why does someone do this? People engage in self-harming behaviors for many reasons, including to escape a feeling, cope with stress, express pain, punish themselves, or feel euphoric. The behaviors can be impulsive or ritualistic. It is a way to make yourself feel better when you believe nothing else will work. And in the very short term, self-harm behaviors typically work. They serve as a way to make the pain less intense (or in some cases just to feel anything). The problem is that self-harm is not an effective long-term solution. Hurting yourself to feel better is likely sad and terrifying. Self-harming is a sign that the other skills to cope (without hurting yourself) aren't strong enough. The solution is to work on developing these other skills so you don't self-harm.

WAYS TO STOP HARMING YOURSELF

Recognize triggers: Typically, people experience an increase in "intolerable" feelings when they are around someone or something that is triggering these feelings. It's important to recognize these triggers to prevent yourself from feeling like the emotions are coming out of nowhere. If you know how they start, then you can make a plan to cope better.

Break rituals: Often, people who self-harm on a regular basis have a ritual or pattern of behavior that is similar each time. This ritual is reinforcing because our brains are wired to like things to be the same, which further contributes to harming yourself. The goal is to break this pattern. For example, if you typically harm yourself when you get back from school, change your after-school routine. Rather than going to your room, stay in the living room and play a phone app/game, or get with a friend until the urge subsides.

> *Anxiety is a sort of byway between possibility and actuality, a necessary anguish one endures in order to grow or develop or improve.*
>
> —Daniel Smith, author of *Monkey Mind*

Change negative thoughts: Do your best to take the negative thought in your head and reframe it in a more positive way. Try to look for the reason why you hurt yourself. For example:

Negative thought: I'm a bad person for cutting myself.

Positive thought: I cut myself because it was the only way I knew how to help myself at the time.

Negative thought: I have no other way to feel better.

Positive thought: At the time I felt like I didn't have any other way to feel better, but there are things I can do for myself that can help.

Reach out to others: It's important to know this isn't something you should try to do on your own. People are scared and ashamed to tell other people because they are afraid they will be judged. If you care enough to tell a specific person, there's a good chance they care enough about you to help, and not judge. Remember, you get to decide who you tell and who you don't. If you don't feel comfortable telling someone in your personal life, you can always contact a professional or clinic. You are allowed to get help on your own! Clinics that work with teenagers are quite familiar with this dilemma and can talk to you about how to help.

Exercise: Exercising is a great way to boost the way you feel. It doesn't have to be a gym, but make sure you are outside moving around. Doing this on a regular basis helps your body to release endorphins and other feel-good brain chemicals.

Find a substitute for cutting: Instead of using a sharp edge, take a piece of ice and hold it where you normally cut your skin. You can also try taking a dark red marker and mark your skin instead of cutting. It works.

A helpful side note: Cutting and borderline personality disorder (BPD) have received a lot of attention in popular culture. Unfortunately, sometimes people with a history of cutting will automatically assume because they cut themselves, they have BPD. An internet search on BPD would likely then cause more anxiety, as the symptoms are intense and it is a difficult diagnosis to treat. Sometimes people think, "If I cut, then I must be a 'borderline.'" This is not true. You cannot be diagnosed with BPD just because you cut yourself. There are many other symptoms that need to be met to be diagnosed with BPD (including being at least 18 years old, which is a requirement for any of the personality disorders).

SUICIDE

Suicide is the act of ending one's own life voluntarily. The reasons for suicide can include depression, psychosis, making a sudden life-altering mistake, impulsivity, or expressing a desire for help in the best way one knows how.

WARNING SIGNS

- Long-term sadness or sudden mood changes.
- A sudden increase in mood after a long period of sadness (the person has decided they will end their life and they feel good about it).
- Sense of hopelessness.
- Abrupt changes in personality.
- Increase in alcohol or drug use.
- Risky behavior or dangerous behavior.
- Making end-of-life preparations, such as giving away personal items, writing a suicide note, or suddenly making amends with someone.
- Telling someone they will kill themselves. According to statistics from the government, 50 to 75 percent of people considering suicide will give a warning sign to someone.
- Someone close to you commits suicide.

Important to know: It does not happen all the time, but often enough. Someone considering suicide will tell a friend, "Can you keep a secret? I'm thinking of killing myself." Out of respect, the friend does not tell anyone, and then feels intense guilt and remorse for not saying anything if that person kills themselves. This is why it is important to tell someone if you have a friend that tells you this. You're not breaking your word. In reality, you are being the best kind of friend.

SUICIDAL THOUGHTS

It's not unusual for people with high amounts of anxiety to have thoughts of suicide. Professionals call these suicidal thoughts ideations. Ideations come in two forms: 1) passive or 2) with intent.

Passive suicidal ideations are thoughts of suicide, but they lack a plan or intention of following through with the thoughts. They are more general and are something like, "I wouldn't actually do it, but sometimes I wish I wasn't here anymore." Teenagers and adults I work with are often surprised to hear that it's not unusual for these types of thoughts to happen. People are often scared and sometimes even embarrassed to tell me because they are concerned that I will judge them in some way.

I am telling you about this because I don't want you to be scared or think that these thoughts are a bad thing. However, they are to be taken seriously, and if you do have thoughts like this I recommend you see a professional as soon as possible. I make this recommendation because the fact that you are thinking this way suggests that something in your life is overwhelming and you are struggling to cope. This is what professionals are trained for. Allow them to help!

THE TEEN ANXIETY GUIDEBOOK

Suicidal thoughts with intent and a plan to end your life are more concerning. If this is how you currently feel, the best option is to call 911 or 988, or have someone take you to the hospital for an assessment ASAP. Remember, it's just an assessment. Professionals are trained at helping people when they feel this way. The person you talk with will listen to why you feel this way and discuss your thoughts of suicide, as well as other information (such as your family history). What happens next depends upon the assessment of the person you talk with, but you will feel supported and understood at each step.

If you are feeling suicidal:

- Call 911 or 988, or have someone take you to an ER.
- Remove any objects from your home that you might use, including firearms. Police stations will hold on to firearms and return them after the suicidal thoughts go away.
- Tell someone you are feeling this way. Often people do not want to tell anyone because they are afraid they will be judged as weak or failing. In actuality, when you tell someone, especially a professional, it can provide a sense of relief. Unloading your burden is helpful, and the professional will guide you through the next steps.
- When you are not feeling actively suicidal, create a safety plan that will give you a guide for what to do, step by step, for when you do feel suicidal. This will allow you to follow along with the steps and not have to rely on higher level rationalization when you're more vulnerable.
- Start/continue to see a mental health professional.

Overall, if you feel that you are engaging in self-harming behaviors or have thoughts of suicide, the most helpful action you can take is to tell someone and receive some professional help. The issues cannot be solved solely by reading this book. This is why mental health professionals exist, and the treatments are effective.

The greater the anxiety the greater the man.

— Søren Kierkegaard

WAYS TO ALLEVIATE ANXIETY

107. Laugh! Go to a comedy show, whether it's an open mic night or The Improv. Or, watch some funny YouTube videos.

108. List the things you're grateful for in a gratitude journal. Then, add to them constantly and reread. A gratitude journal is simply a diary of things for which you are grateful. The benefits of focusing on gratitude are numerous and include making you happier; making you healthier; making you more effective, productive, and successful; making you more attractive to others; increasing your social circle; making you more optimistic and hopeful; increasing your self-esteem; creating a better present and better memories; and many more. Or, use one of a number of great phone apps to track and list the things you feel gratitude for throughout the day.

109. Look at videos of soldiers returning home and surprising their children or pets (it's calming and heartwarming).

110. Mess around with the camera settings on your phone. Try to make an ordinary object look good in the photo, or use filters to make an ordinary picture look extraordinary, and save it.

111. Figure out how to get a photo of your whole body jumping in the air, without any assistance.

112. See how many push-ups or sit-ups you can do in one minute.

113. Search for inspirational quotes on the internet. The ones in this book don't count!

CHAPTER 15

CAUSE AND EFFECT OF LONG-TERM ANXIETY

Now is the age of anxiety.

—W. H. Auden

DON'T FEED WILD ANXIETIES

In case you forgot what good company you're in, anxiety disorders are the most common mental ailment in the US. Anxiety and depression have come to the forefront in recent years due to less stigma and an overall acceptance of mental disorders. It's hard to keep something sequestered when it causes misery to tens of millions of Americans. Suffering from anxiety is often seen as the cost of living a busy, productive lifestyle. And if you don't have a debilitating amount, then you might be perceived as lacking enough responsibility.

There is also the deluge of TV and magazine advertisements for anxiety and antidepressant meds. I find that whenever I mention taking the meds to someone, half the time they eagerly retort with what anxiety meds they themselves are taking. Looking back on our time in history, it might one day be called the Age of Anxiety, where the speed and stressors of life blindsided us before we developed the cerebral skills to manage the related advances. Anxiety disorders are highly treatable; but, sadly, only about one-third of those suffering receive some form of treatment. Anxiety loves to run wild and unfettered while feeding on unwary serene minds. Anxiety is an opportunistic asshole.

MANAGE THE SPIKES AND RELAPSES

I don't think of my anxiety in terms of "recovery and relapse." Like a cowlick, anxiety is always present. I don't worry about it coming back since it lacks the common courtesy to leave. For me, anxiety relapse prevention means keeping anxiety at a manageable level at all times by using the skills we cover in this book. Oftentimes my anxiety is nothing more than streaming background chatter in my head. If I don't consistently manage it, the negative chatter gets louder, the anxiety increases, and depression hitches a ride.

If someone wants to call me the anxious girl, depressed girl, or girl with mental disorders, that's fine. In time, they'll find that the anxious girl is pretty cool.
—Harmony Rose Rogers, individual with mental illness

The signs for anxiety relapse will differ from person to person but can include any of the following: mood changes; irritability; loss of concentration; withdrawal from friends and social engagements; irrational or hostile behaviors; poor hygiene and lack of self-care; changes in diet; and changes in sleep patterns. There are common factors that can lead to anxiety relapse, such as not adhering to medication protocols, drug and alcohol abuse, lack of sleep, loneliness, health issues, and academic or job stress.

I have a trusty formula to manage my anxiety and prevent spikes that involves using some preferred coping skills. My formulary is a mix of tactics we've reviewed thus far, but includes regular usage of specific anti-relapse or anxiety spike tools:

1. Acknowledge your anxiety. Denying it will only anger it, and anxiety is an attention whore.

2. Stay rooted in the present moment. Don't look back, and don't look forward. You can only be here. Now.

3. Pay attention to breathing. Breathing changes everything. Anxiety hates when you breathe normally. It wants you to hyperventilate and give it all your attention.

4. Channel nervous energy into something creative daily.

5. Monitor thoughts continuously while challenging/disputing the negative thoughts.

6. Practice gratitude daily. This can include citing at least three things for which you're thankful that day.

7. Sleep! Go to bed early during the week in particular. If you're anxiety prone, you probably like to stay up late and watch TV, play on your phone, wake your friends, and do anything

but fall asleep. This makes for rough mornings and rougher days. It's not uncommon for me to hit the snooze button on my alarm for 90 minutes if I don't get to bed by 10 p.m. You can't shut off your mind if you're feeding it stimuli. Turn off the electronics and turn off your brain.

8. Always have a productivity goal (something from your To-Do list) and a pleasure goal (something from your Fun-To-Do list) in place. This can be a fun hike on a weekend, a getaway, time with friends, or a movie; it doesn't matter how small. Just keep them coming.

9. Socialize! Anxiety is selfish and wants you all to itself, especially if that means isolating you away from other humans so you have nothing else to dwell on other than your misery.

10. Eat well and get regular exercise. Go easy on the caffeine, eat your veggies, and get outside or to the gym.

11. Counter anxiety. Whatever anxiety is urging you to do—do the opposite. If it wants you to lock the door 48 times, lock it once slowly and purposefully and walk away. And if it wants you to stay home and avoid the school dance, go dance! Anxiety can't dance.

Love yourself for who you are—anxiety and all. In fact, give your anxiety a big ole hug. The sooner you get acquainted, the better.

These are my go-to tactics on any given day—except dancing, which I avoid due to a gross lack of rhythm. I also leverage many other skills, as needed, from those listed throughout this book. Dr. McDonagh covers more techniques and exercises to prevent relapse starting on page 244. With a little experimentation, you will choose your own favorites to effectively counter anxiety. The key to effectively managing chronic anxiety and preventing spikes or relapses is regular application of the skills you've seen thus far.

For most of us, anxiety will ebb and flow depending on life circumstances or a complete lack of explanation. But you are no longer powerless to mitigate the effects. In addition to the 101 items peppered throughout this book to help you conquer your anxiety, it's our hope that you discover your own favorite skills from which to choose quickly whenever anxiety increases or comes back. No longer does anxiety need to determine outcomes for you. Make a conscious decision now, before you close this book, to flip your life script. In this revised personal story, you are the hero, the victor, the happy protagonist, and the one to whom the spoils flow. In the story of your life, the influence and character of Anxiety becomes the insignificant credit of Antagonist.

I spent my teen years hating my anxiety and wondering if it would be my demise. This was all before I acknowledged having it, learned to manage the anxiety rather than be managed by it, and realized that my neurosis is also what drives my creative energy. Even when my anxiety peaks today, I'm not ashamed of being anxious and make no apologies for it. If your anxiety is driving the train, talk to your conductor.

SHOW ANXIETY WHAT'S UP

Since we have an average of 50,000 thoughts per day, it's key to positively frame as many of them as possible while challenging the rest. As you've learned by now, long-term negative thinking can develop attitudes and behaviors that can be extremely difficult to stop or overcome once they gain momentum, even creating problems that don't exist, like feeling the need to iron your bed sheets.

It's our hope that you've learned some things about your anxiety by this point. Although I have a long history of anxiety, I cannot know everything you're feeling. I can only surmise based on my own feelings, past and present. The first half of my life was rampant and nearly ruined by anxiety because I had only anxiety and none of the coping skills. The second half is where I learned everything necessary to counter my anxiety and feel happy again. I don't have less anxiety today than as a teen. I have just as much. But it feels like a fraction of what I had as a teen. Why? Because I learned to dampen its negative effects and accentuate the positive (creative) side. I'm not doing anything that you can't be doing. Conversely, Dr. McDonagh and I wrote this book so you will have the skills necessary to show anxiety what's up.

Maybe your anxiety will go away never to be seen again, maybe it won't. There's no way for us to know. Anxiety doesn't always go away; but it can always be controlled. Your salvation lies in knowing that no matter how bad it might get, it's still completely manageable.

It's not a choice. You don't choose to have anxiety. It chooses you.

—Patricia Lynn

Preventing spikes or relapses of anxiety also includes setting realistic expectations. So, going forward, don't be afraid to set those boundaries we discussed, and tell others what they need to know if they wish to remain in your sphere of influence. It's far better to set parameters and expectations up front than to get anxious and possibly blow up later. Trust me, I've lost more friends than I can recall by not being up front and true to myself, then lashing out in an anxious frenzy later. As an anxious person, you have needs that are different from others. And that's okay! Pay attention to those things or it will lead to frustration. If nothing else, when you're going through a storm, someone's silent presence is more powerful than a million empty words.

Here are some helpful statements you can practice using that will help:

- I don't want to go, and that's okay.
- I set my own pace. It's okay if you don't follow my beat.
- I know that my worries and fears don't make sense to you. They don't make sense to me either. But that doesn't mean they're not real.
- I'm doing my best with the skills I have at any given moment.
- Yes, I know I hate change—but I'm trying.
- Yes, I can get irritable or moody. So, if I tell you I need to be alone, it's for your own good.
- Excuse me while I try to accept my inner turmoil and settle into my own skin. This takes time.

- Rather than criticize me, how about asking how you can help?
- Walk this walk with me, or walk away. I need people who've got my back like I have yours.
- I care; I'm just practicing some healthy apathy. The less I care about what others think or say about me, the better off I am.
- Rather than giving me things to worry about, feel free to share possibilities with me.
- You may not know this, but it's perfectly okay to be an anxious person or have depression. It's actually "normal."
- Please don't judge me; I'm a work in progress.

- Yes, I'm tired. Trying to conceptually figure everything out can be exhausting.

ANXIETY AND CREATIVITY

The best use of imagination is creativity. The worst use of imagination is anxiety.

—Deepak Chopra

The main difference between overthinkers and the rest of the population is imagination. It is likely that you've noticed that the backside of your anxiety is some notable imagination and creativity. I used to wonder a lot about this and ran a Google search of "famous people with anxiety." The findings include an array of creative artists that include Emma Stone, Jennifer Lawrence, Sarah Silverman, Beyonce, Taylor Swift, Mara Wilson, Lena Dunham, Adele, Amanda Seyfried, Chris Evans, Kirsten Stewart, Kate Moss, John Mayer, Britney Spears, Demi Lovato, Dakota Johnson, Colton Haynes, Johnny Depp, Nicole Kidman, Jessica Alba, Ireland Baldwin, Olivia Munn, Zach Braff, Cameron Diaz, Charlize Theron, Cher, Howie Mandel, Courtney Love, Naomi Campbell, Alanis Morissette, Nicolas Cage, Sheryl Crow, Winona Ryder, Scarlett Johansson, Christina Ricci, Jim Carrey, Drew Barrymore, Halle Berry, Chloë Sevigny, Angelina Jolie, Miley Cyrus, Amanda Bynes, Lady Gaga, Selena Gomez, and so many more. The list gets much longer when you add "depression" to the search string. And if you itemized all the celebrities with anxiety or depression, you would have a list of nearly every creative artist you can imagine. One might even assume it's only the "cool kids" who have anxiety or depression. But it's the opposite— it's the anxiety that leads people to channel their creative energy and pursue the arts. Tap into it. It's real.

The Unexpected Benefits of Anxiety

Interestingly, anxiety can have unique upsides. For me, anxiety further ensured that I'd never become a conformist. I have not followed a traditional path in life. I never put a priority on getting married, having kids, or making buckets of money. I still don't. People I meet marvel at this as if I'm some rogue oddity who needs to fall back into line. I almost believed this myself a few times. As a teen, I hated not fitting into any preconceived concept, but I'm grateful about that today.

Another benefit anxiety has given me is a "sixth sense" that makes me more in tune with everyone and everything around me on an intense level. It's a sense I never wanted, but use to my advantage. This deep perception is half intuitive mental radar (hypervigilance) that scans my environment for potential threats 24/7, and half an ability to read people extremely quickly while establishing rapport with the ones that matter. I can get a read on strangers quite fast, and it's typically spot on.

The concept of being in a constant state of hypervigilance is a common one for anxiety sufferers. You might better know it as your Spidey Sense. Always trust your first gut instincts.

The anxiety/creativity relationship is supported by science. Psychology researchers have made a connection between anxiety and a stronger imagination. Neuroticism and anxiety have both costs and benefits. The findings were presented in the August 2015 Trends in Cognitive Sciences. Dr. Adam Perkins, a lecturer in Neurobiology of Personality at King's College London and one of the paper's authors, told *The Huffington Post* that "Highly neurotic people will suffer a lot of anxiety and depression over their lifespan, but their deep-thinking, brooding tendencies can also give rise to greater creative potential."

The authors argue that the part of the brain responsible for self-generated thought is highly active in neuroticism, which yields both of the trait's positives (e.g., creativity) and negatives (e.g., misery). The overthinking hypothesis also explains the positives of neuroticism. The creativity of Isaac Newton and other neurotics may simply be the result of their tendency to dwell on problems far longer than average people.

"We're still a long way off from fully explaining neuroticism, and we're not offering all of the answers, but we hope that our new theory will help people make sense of their own experiences, and show that although being highly neurotic is by definition unpleasant, it also has creative benefits," Dr. Perkins states.

YOU HAVE YOUR OWN PACE. FOLLOW IT.

The shortest route to unhappiness is to compare oneself to others.

Regarding your progress with managing anxiety, the only one you should be comparing yourself to is you. Benchmark yourself against where you were before you started working on your anxiety. In the end, that's all that matters. It doesn't matter what anyone else is doing or how well they're doing it. All that matters is if you are learning and improving as you go. I can tell you that the most redemptive feeling I've ever had was the moment I stopped measuring myself against others who I thought were happier, richer, and stronger, had more cats, etc. Some of the ability to do this comes with age, but not all. If you can harness the power in doing this now, it will change your life. Dramatically. Life is a process where you continually hone yourself against your former self. And it never stops. That's why you'll rarely hear any adult say, "I wish I were 16 again!" Because we don't! Why? Because there is so much learning, internal peace, and self-confidence gathered along the way that most people aren't willing to trade that progress for anything, including their former hairline or Olympian knees. You've got a lot to look forward to and much happiness to gain from learning. Try to do it while you still get carded at movies.

The point is that you need to be true to you. If a little voice in your head is guiding you toward certain paths, it's likely for good reason. The problem exists when you butt up against your life purpose to settle on money, what society defines as successful, or because it has a nice title. Follow your own path. If that's running a macaroon cart in Morocco, great! Be true to yourself, your passions, and your dreams. Being the best version of you is commendable.

> *Be yourself. No one can say you're doing it wrong.*
> —Charles M. Schulz

DR. TOM'S TAKE

RELAPSE PREVENTION

As Jon and I have said throughout this book, the goal is never to remove anxiety, because that is impossible. Our goal is to bring anxiety down to more manageable levels. What that means moving forward is that there will be times when you experience a random spike in your anxiety. Do not worry. These random spikes are part of the healing process and are normal. Having some anxiety return, either randomly or triggered, does not mean that you are starting back from step one all over again. It just means you're having some anxiety at that particular moment. Again, this is normal and what is expected to happen. Life can be anxiety provoking at times.

> *It's a disorder, not a decision.*

As you begin to have greater control over your anxiety, there are some things you can do to help manage these spikes. Remind yourself of the core skills for controlling your body and your thoughts:

Breathing: Nice, controlled breaths where you breathe in for four seconds and back out for four seconds. We do this because anxiety makes us want to unconsciously breathe faster, which makes our anxiety worse. When you are breathing in, imagine the air going all the way down to the bottom of your lungs. This deeper breathing will make you use your diaphragm, which is what you want. If you need to, place one hand on your chest and one hand on your stomach. You will know you are using your diaphragm when you feel your hands slightly going up and down, opposite of each other.

Get better at 4x4 breathing: Four seconds breathing in, four seconds breathing out, by doing it three times a day, for five minutes each time. Do it even when you do not feel anxious. The goal is to get so good at it that it becomes muscle memory and you are able to do it on the spot when you are feeling anxious. It takes time to develop muscle memory, so keep at it. You have to breathe anyway, right?

Progressive muscle relaxation: This is where you contract certain muscle groups for 10 to 15 seconds, and then release the muscle and allow it to rest for 10 to 15 seconds. Then, move on to the next muscle group. Be sure to focus on what it feels like for certain muscle groups to be tense, but also what it feels like for them to be relaxed. Muscle groups to focus on can include your hands, arms, feet, lower legs, upper legs, core, shoulder, and facial areas. There are many guided scripts you can follow on the internet. Search for "progressive muscle relaxation" or "Jacobson relaxation technique." The goal is to help you feel less stressed in the moment, but also to help you catch yourself in the future when you unconsciously tense muscles like your shoulders or jaw because of anxiety.

List of 101 options: Scan the list for self-soothing techniques that you think would be most helpful for you in the moment. Hint: Splashing cold water on your face is an easily available and pretty reliable option for some quick help to make you feel less edgy.

Let's start the process right now.

UNCONSCIOUS, WORST-CASE SCENARIOS

Remember, anxious thoughts are always going to be triggered by an unconscious, worst-case scenario. Do your best to uncover what this worst-case scenario is, and then come up with a challenging statement.

For example:

Anxious thought: I am going to fail this test.

Unconscious, worst-case scenario: If I fail this test, then I won't get into college, and my life is over.

Challenging statement: I studied, and usually when I study I do at least well enough. Plus, one test is not going to ruin my life.

ACTIVITY
Challenge Anxious Thoughts

Below are some common anxious thoughts. See if you can fill out the underlying worst-case scenario, and then provide a challenging statement.

Anxious thought: I need to do well when I'm in the game today.

Unconscious, worst-case scenario:

_____

_____

Challenging statement:

_____

_____

Anxious thought: I can't believe I got dumped.

Unconscious, worst-case scenario:

_____

_____

Challenging statement:

_____

_____

Anxious thought: I didn't get invited to the party.

Unconscious, worst-case scenario:

_____

_____

Challenging statement:

_____

_____

Anxious thought: I don't want to have sex.

Unconscious, worst-case scenario:

_____

_____

Challenging statement:

_____

_____

Anxious thought: I didn't get into my number one college.

Unconscious, worst-case scenario:

_____

_____

Challenging statement:

_____

_____

PERSONAL WARNING SIGNS

It takes work, especially in the beginning, to maintain a life that is free of unnecessary worry. It's easy over time to let your efforts slip. There's lots to do during the day, life happens, and as your anxiety begins to improve, it becomes something that you think less about. And that's when people fall back into old habits and the anxiety begins to return.

It's okay to try and fail. It's okay to try and succeed. And it's okay to try and fail, and try and fail, and try and fail. Keep trying.
—Dr. Tom McDonagh

Unfortunately, making your anxiety go away is not like learning how to ride a bike that once you learn, you don't have to figure out how to do ever again. Rather, having an anxiety-free life is like learning how to ride a bike anew every day. Yes, it does get easier over time, but try to keep the bike metaphor in mind. As a result, it's important to be aware of your personal warning signs for anxiety and have a plan to recommit to using your skills to improve your mood.

Your Anxiety Management Plan

Follow along below to help develop your plan for anxiety management.

I know I am at risk for a return in my anxiety when I have the following warning signs:

1. _____

2. _____

3. _____

4. _____

Rank your warning signs in order from most worrisome to least worrisome:

1. _____

2. _____

3. _____

4. _____

Pick the top two most worrisome warning signs and fill out the following worksheet for them:

Warning sign #1

When I experience this warning sign ...

I tend to think:

_____

I tend to feel:

_____

I have an urge to:

_____

What I actually do is:

_____

I can manage these thoughts by:

_____

Cause and Effect of Long-Term Anxiety

I can manage these feelings by:

_____

I can manage these urges by:

_____

Warning sign #2

When I experience this warning sign …

I tend to think:

_____

I tend to feel:

_____

I have an urge to:

_____

What I actually do is:

_____

I can manage these thoughts by:

_____

I can manage these feelings by:

_____

I can manage these urges by:

_____

Continue to revisit the skills and topics discussed in this book. If you are anything like me, a once-over read isn't enough. To really grasp and remember information, I need to reread it several times. Do so as necessary with this book, and go back to the skills and topics as often as needed.

114. Practice some visualization or mental imagery. It's really nothing more than imagining success. You've likely already dipped into this technique whenever you've imagined yourself as a pro athlete, renowned artist, famous singer, well-known actor, or leading scholar. People who have achieved greatness first spent time visualizing it through mental imagery. Basically, whatever it is that you want to achieve—whether a personal record on a 10k, a flawless golf swing, a recital, or a knock-out presentation—visualize yourself doing it successfully. According to scientists, such envisioning elicits nervous-system responses comparable to those recorded during physical execution of the imagined action.

115. Learn a card trick.

116. Take a bath. Use fragrant and calming bath bombs or salts.

117. Hold an ice cube on your tongue until it melts.

118. Organize a street hockey, volleyball, basketball, or touch football game with friends.

119. Play tennis/handball/racquetball, or try to get better at serving in any of the aforementioned.

120. Recite the Serenity Prayer (see page 26). Slowly.

121. Send a friend/family member a postcard, or the lost art of the handwritten letter.

Chapter 16

101+ WAYS TO ALLEVIATE ANXIETY QUICKLY

The best way out is always through.

—Robert Frost

Anxiety disorders are the most common mental illness in the US, affecting 40 million adults in the United States age 18 and older, or 18 percent of the population. To reiterate, this staggering number precludes people under age 18.

Happiness takes practice, effort, and observance. It doesn't happen on its own. Feeling anxious is a great impetus for needed change. Anxiety can be used as a point of introspection and change in life direction. It's the perfect time to take personal inventory and change jobs, end or begin relationships, take on new healthy habits or hobbies, etc.

If you are suffering from anxiety, you have two choices: You can manage the anxiety, or let it manage you. If you're reading this book, you're not a quitter—you'll be the one doing the managing. So, let's review some ways to eliminate or at least reduce the bad feelings by first accepting your emotions and knowing you have a choice, and then taking some simple actions to counter the anxiety itself.

Keep in mind that it's absolutely possible to ease your anxiety and even cure chronic anxiety forever. In the interim, however, the following coping techniques will help to decrease the effects of your anxiety, making it far more manageable.

CHAPTER 1 WAYS TO ALLEVIATE ANXIETY

1. Accept that you are anxious in order to lessen it.

2. Rearrange the furniture in your room.

3. Write it out in a diary or journal.

4. Challenge your anxious thoughts and beliefs. What is the evidence? What is the worst case? What is likely?

5. Practice desensitization.

6. Confront the sources of your anxiety. Change what you can. Accept what you cannot.

7. Install some anxiety-related apps on your smartphone, and carry anxiety relief with you.

8. Get a touchstone.

CHAPTER 2 WAYS TO ALLEVIATE ANXIETY

9. Time how long you can hold your breath, and work to beat your previous time each attempt.

10. Learn how to cook or bake something that is somewhat challenging.

11. Listen to a podcast or TED talk.

12. Look up something new about art. Even better, visit your local museum.

13. Roll tennis balls under your bare feet. It feels great!

14. Chew gum. Make it sugarless.

15. Use meditation rather than medication, where applicable (prescription or otherwise).

16. Hug it out.

CHAPTER 3 WAYS TO ALLEVIATE ANXIETY

17. Practice mindfulness. Root yourself in the present moment, accepting it without judgment and looking neither to the past nor future. Mindfulness is a form of meditation and a key element of happiness.

18. Go for a walk or a hike, preferably in a park or nature setting. Being in nature is a fast remedy for anxiety.

19. Limit your time on social media. Since you can't control some of the asinine posts from "friends," you can limit your exposure.

20. Stop comparing yourself to others. Doing so is one of the quickest routes to unhappiness and stress. Take solace in knowing that you are right where you need to be at this moment. Your life and course are yours alone.

21. Use calming oils (aka aromatherapy) such as lavender. Consider using a small diffuser. It may seem trite and pointless, but it works well. Inhaling the aroma from the essential oils of flowers, bark, stems, leaves, and roots is widely believed to stimulate brain function and enhance psychological well-being.

22. Take a day trip. It could mean getting out of your typical surroundings to somewhere you enjoy, either alone or with a friend/loved one.

23. See how far you can stretch. Work to become more flexible. Anxiety typically has us in knots. Literally.

24. Go to the batting cages.

CHAPTER 4 WAYS TO ALLEVIATE ANXIETY

25. Call your grandparents or go talk to an older neighbor. Ask them about their childhood.

26. Think of a happy moment in your life and dwell on it for a bit.

27. Do your laundry (it's actually relaxing!), or unload the dishwasher/help clean the dishes.

28. Read a book or magazine.

29. Put your hand on whatever object is in front of you. Write down as many different words as you can to describe what that object feels like under your hand.

30. Listen to music you love.

31. Go on a bike ride.

32. Learn how to say something very weird in a different language (e.g., "I don't like to eat soup with my tweed vest on" or "Cold feet make me think slowly").

CHAPTER 5 WAYS TO ALLEVIATE ANXIETY

33. Get organized. Clean your room, organize your closet, write that research paper, etc.

34. Know and accept that your anxiety will pass. Accept it as it waxes and wanes over and through you.

35. Go outside, find a bird, and try to identify it.

36. Stare gently at a spot on the floor for five minutes. Observe what happens to your vision and thoughts.

37. Splash cold water on your face.

38. Write a list of your skills and strengths.

39. Remind yourself that you are doing the best you can for where you are at this moment. Because that's the truth.

40. Doodle or sketch.

CHAPTER 6 WAYS TO ALLEVIATE ANXIETY

41. Tell that secret someone that you like them.

42. Learn to juggle.

43. Search through all the different emojis on your phone. Don't stop until you've looked at every single one. Try not to rush.

44. Put on a song, and dance.

45. Get social. Spend time with a few close friends and family members.

46. Get a foot massage, body massage, mani-pedi, or haircut.

47. Phone a friend—even when you don't want to.

48. Learn a new form of exercise, such as pilates, spinning, or a kettlebell workout.

CHAPTER 7 WAYS TO ALLEVIATE ANXIETY

49. Begin learning a new language.

50. Volunteer.

51. Find a hill and run up, then walk down, repeating this until you are tired.

52. Walk into a room; in one minute, try to memorize exactly how it looks. When the minute is up, walk into a different room and draw or write down the image you have in your mind.

53. Make a paper airplane travel as far as possible.

54. Learn how to flip a pen around your thumb.

55. Try to memorize 20 anxiety-reducing tactics from this book.

56. Memorize a few lines or a paragraph of a famous speech or monologue.

CHAPTER 8 WAYS TO ALLEVIATE ANXIETY

57. Question the validity of your anxiety.

58. Put a piece of chocolate in your mouth and see how long you can keep it there before you bite into it.

59. Learn to throw a knuckleball or fast-pitch a softball.

60. Throw a Frisbee with someone.

61. Learn to drive a manual transmission (if you're old enough).

62. Learn how to do a handstand or cartwheel.

63. Implement some simple breathing exercises, like 4x4 breathing (see page 134).

64. Get busy. Do something—anything.

CHAPTER 9 WAYS TO ALLEVIATE ANXIETY

65. Get outside or go to the window and look out at the horizon.

66. Try using an adult coloring book. They're pretty fun!

67. Learn to say hello in as many languages as you can.

68. Pop any bubble wrap that you have around your house. Try to take a deep breath after each pop.

69. Envision what your role model would tell you about how to cope with this moment.

70. Try dimming the lights of your room to provide a different stimulus.

71. Learn a magic trick with playing cards.

72. Teach your family dog (or pet) a new trick.

73. Try to garden outside. Or just get your hands dirty and pull up some weeds.

74. Try to find new music or a band you might like.

CHAPTER 10 WAYS TO ALLEVIATE ANXIETY

75. Take a cold shower.

76. Invite a friend over to watch a comedy movie.

77. Learn to crochet.

78. Spend some time with your family pet.

79. Make a playlist of songs you like and plan to share it with a friend.

80. Shoot some hoops.

81. Use your phone to identify the constellations of the stars at night.

82. Make yourself a smoothie.

83. Complete a crossword puzzle.

84. Wrap a cold washcloth over your forehead for five minutes.

CHAPTER 11 WAYS TO ALLEVIATE ANXIETY

85. Google "celebrities with anxiety."

86. Get creative. Channel your nervous energy into an outlet such as painting, writing, sculpting, acting, music, design, dance, or film production.

87. See a therapist for guidance.

88. Go to the gym, or join a spin or yoga class.

89. Play a video game—even if you're not a gamer.

90. Take a B-complex vitamin. These nutrients are depleted first when you're anxious or stressed.

91. Eat healthfully!

92. Learn a new sport, like field hockey, lacrosse, kiteboarding, etc.

CHAPTER 12 WAYS TO ALLEVIATE ANXIETY

93. Pick a goal, and go after it.

94. Teach yourself to snap a bottle cap.

95. Shuffle a deck of cards over and over (it's soothing.)

96. Start positive self-talk to counter negative chatter ("I feel terrible now, but I will overcome this!").

97. Schedule your worry time and postpone all worry until that 30-minute assigned time.

98. Find a self-defense/martial arts/MMA class and do a free trial.

99. Do as many freestanding body squats as you're able.

CHAPTER 13 WAYS TO ALLEVIATE ANXIETY

100. Download a soothing meditative sound app.

101. Floss your teeth.

102. Put your phone in a different room, a drawer, closet, car trunk, etc. See how long you can entertain yourself without looking at it.

103. Using a pencil, try to shade a piece of paper evenly, going from very dark to very light.

104. List as many cities in the US that you can. Don't stop until the only things you can think of are cities.

105. Take a fish oil supplement.

106. Memorize a Bible/Koran/Torah/scripture verse or the lyrics to a favorite song.

CHAPTER 14 WAYS TO ALLEVIATE ANXIETY

107. Laugh! Go to a comedy show, whether it be an open mic night or a headliner at The Improv. Or, watch some funny YouTube videos.

108. List the things you're grateful for in a gratitude journal. Then, add to them constantly and reread.

109. Look at videos of soldiers returning home and surprising their children or pets (it's calming and heartwarming).

110. Mess around with the camera settings on your phone. Try to make an ordinary object look good in the photo, or use filters to make an ordinary picture look extraordinary, and save it.

111. Figure out how to get a photo of your whole body jumping in the air, without any assistance.

112. See how many push-ups or sit-ups you can do in one minute.

113. Search for inspirational quo~~~ ~~~e on~
book don't count!

114. Practice some visualization or mental imagery. It's really nothing more than imagining success.

115. Learn a card trick.

116. Take a bath.

117. Hold an ice cube on your tongue until it melts.

118. Organize a street hockey, volleyball, basketball, or touch football game with friends.

119. Play tennis/handball/racquetball, or try to get better at serving in any of the aforementioned.

120. Recite the Serenity Prayer (see page 26). Slowly.

121. Send a friend/family member a postcard, or the lost art of the handwritten letter.

Begin to weave and God will give you the thread.

—German proverb

REFERENCES

American Psychiatric Association. *Diagnostic and Statistical Manual of Mental Disorders*, 5th ed. Arlington, VA: American Psychiatric Association.

American Psychological Association. "Children, Youth, Families and Socioeconomic Status." Accessed May 2, 2016. https://www.apa.org /pi/ses/resources/publications/factsheet-cyf.aspx.

Anxiety and Depression Society of America. "Sleep Disorders." Accessed May 2, 2016. https://www.adaa.org/understanding-anxiety /related-illnesses/sleep-disorders.

Burns, David D. *Feeling Good: The New Mood Therapy*. New York: HarperCollins, 1980.

Citizens Commission on Human Rights. "Psychiatry: Hooking Your World on Drugs." Accessed May 2, 2016. https://www.cchr.org/cchr -reports/psychiatry/introduction.html.

Davey, Graham C. L. "The Psychological Effects of TV News." *Psychology Today* (June 19, 2012). https://www.psychologytoday.com /blog/why-we-worry/201206/the-psychological-effects-tv-news.

Hugo, N. "Children as Agents of Change for the Future," in *Children in Sustainable and Responsible Tourism*, ed. Séraphin, H. (Bingley, UK: Emerald Publishing Limited, 2022), 189–99.

Johnston, Wendy M., and Graham C. L. Davey. "The Psychological Impact of Negative TV News Bulletins: The Catastrophizing of Personal Worries." *British Journal of Psychology* 88, no. 1 (February 1997): 85–91. https://onlinelibrary.wiley.com/doi/10.1111/j.2044 -8295.1997.tb02622.x/abstract.

Marchand, W. R. "Mindfulness-Based Stress Reduction, Mindfulness-Based Cognitive Therapy, and Zen Meditation for Depression, Anxiety, Pain, and Psychological Distress." *Journal of Psychiatric Practice* 4 (July 18, 2012): 233–52. https://doi.org/10.1097/01.pra.0000416014 .53215.86.

McHugh, Kathryn R., Sarah W. Whitton, Andrew D. Peckham, et al. "Patient Preference for Psychological vs. Pharmacological Treatment of Psychiatric Disorders: A Meta-Analytic Review." *Journal of Clinical Psychiatry* 74, no. 6 (June 2013): 595–602. http://www.ncbi.nlm.nih .gov/pmc/articles/PMC4156137/pdf/nihms-623724.pdf.

National Center on Addiction and Substance Abuse. "National Study Reveals: Teen Substance Use America's #1 Public Health Problem." June 29, 2011. https://www.centeronaddiction.org/newsroom/press -releases/national-study-reveals-teen-substance-use-americas-1 -public-health-problem.

National Highway Traffic Safety Administration. "Traffic Safety Facts 2013 Data: Young Drivers." October 2015. http://www-nrd.nhtsa.dot .gov/Pubs/812200.pdf.

National Institute of Mental Health. "Anxiety Disorders." Last modified March 2016. https://www.nimh.nih.gov/health/topics /anxiety-disorders/index.

Penney, Alexander M., Victoria C. Miedema, and Dwight Mazmanian. "Intelligence and Emotional Disorders: Is the Worrying and Ruminating Mind a More Intelligent Mind?" *Science Direct* (February 2015). https://doi.org/10.1016/j.paid.2014.10.005.

Riesman, Abraham, and Melissa Dahl. "Watch This Video to Find Out How Anxiety Can Make You Smarter." *New York Magazine* (December 10, 2015). https://nymag.com/scienceofus/2015/12/video-how-anxiety -can-make-you-smarter.html#.

Rosin, Hanna. "The Silicon Valley Suicides: Why Are So Many Kids with Bright Prospects Killing Themselves in Palo Alto?" *The Atlantic*

(December 2015). https://www.theatlantic.com/magazine/archive/2015/12/the-silicon-valley-suicides/413140/.shtml.

Sampasa-Kanyinga, Hugues, and Rosamund F. Lewis. "Frequent Use of Social Networking Sites Is Associated with Poor Psychological Functioning Among Children and Adolescents." *Cyberpsychology, Behavior, and Social Networking* 18, no. 7 (July 2015): 380–85. https://doi.org/10.1089/cyber.2015.0055.

Singal, Jesse. "What All This Bad News Is Doing to Us." *New York Magazine* (August 8, 2014). https://nymag.com/scienceofus/2014/08/what-all-this-bad-news-is-doing-to-us.html.

Szabo, A., and K. L. Hopkinson. "Negative Psychological Effects of Watching the News in the Television: Relaxation or Another Intervention May Be Needed to Buffer Them!" *International Journal of Behavioral Medicine* 14, no. 2 (2007): 57–62. https://www.ncbi.nlm.nih.gov/pubmed/17926432.

Taylor, Steve. "The Jumpers: What Happens When a Person Survives Jumping off the Golden Gate Bridge." *Psychology Today* (September 29, 2011). https://www.psychologytoday.com/blog/out-the-darkness/201109/the-jumpers.

U.S. National Library of Medicine. "Bullying." Accessed January, 5, 2016. https://www.nlm.nih.gov/medlineplus/bullying.html.

ACKNOWLEDGMENTS

As is often the case in life, we can't do it alone. And so, the writing of this book would not have been possible without the support of many individuals.

Firstly, I'd like to thank my parents, Tom and Diane, and my brother, Ryan. Your unconditional love and support have always inspired me to be kind to others and reach for the impossible. I don't know what I did to deserve it, but I am thankful every day to have you in my life. Words fail to express what my family means to me.

The road to earning a doctorate is long, but through the years I have been fortunate to learn from some amazingly talented educators in the university and clinical settings. To these mentors and supervisors at Manhattan College, Nova Southeastern University, Vanderbilt University, and Kaiser Permanente Santa Rosa, thank you. Your guidance during those impressionable years will never be forgotten.

I'd also like to thank my cowriter, Jon. His work ethic is unmatched and his passion is inspiring. Everyone should be so lucky to have their own Jon in their lives.

To Peter, our illustrator, thank you. You joined a project that was still in the development stage, with full force and enthusiasm. You are a creative talent, and we are fortunate to have your contributions in this book.

Finally, I'd like to thank our editor, Renee Rutledge, and the team at Ulysses Press. Renee is an educator in her own right, mentoring Jon and myself through this process with confidence and support. We cannot thank you enough.

—Dr. Thomas McDonagh

Thank you, James and JoAnn Hatcher, for loving me through a lifetime of anxiety, despite all of its perplexing nuances. There simply aren't enough Mother's/Father's Day gifts to compensate you. Thank you for domesticating and wrangling me into the man I've become. I will never love two humans more.

To Maria Ananchenko, my progress and well-being are a testament to your unwavering support. I owe you a house or a Bugatti.

A heart-swelling thank you to Marian Lamb for a lifetime of mission-critical support. Words fail to sufficiently convey my gratitude for your selfless dedication and impartial wisdom. This book and my ability to overcome the absurd would not be possible without you. You are my ambassador to cerebral wellness and diplomat to Rational Mind.

To Dave Peterson, thank you for 27 years of camaraderie and mentorship. You've gifted me with increased peace of mind during trials, and you personify God's love. Through example and teachings, you have helped mold a drifter into a disciple. If asked to limit your description to a single word, it would be "inspirawesomazing."

Thank you, Tom McDonagh, for your knowledge, friendship, and dedication to the State of Anxiety collaboration. And thank you for a lack of discernible anxiety, as only one of us can be neurotic. I look forward to future endeavors and saving humanity with you—one anxious psyche at a time.

Thank you Claire Sielaff, Renee Rutledge, Keith Riegert, and Ulysses Press for recognizing the importance of, and specifically addressing, teen anxiety. Your devotion to the well-being of our youth is notable and praiseworthy. Young minds are the single greatest resource of the future. Renee, thank you for making the publishing process so seamless, enjoyable, and positive. You set the bar.

Peter Brown, our illustrator extraordinaire, thank you for adding your artistry, vigor, and talent to the anxious fray. You've given a cartoon face to teenage angst. You make anxiety fun—almost.

And to our readers, thank you for trusting and affording us the opportunity to impart our knowledge and experience with you in the hopes that you obtain the happiness that is your birthright. Perhaps more than anyone, I know exactly what you're feeling. I've been where you are. No matter how bleak you might feel at any given moment, it will shift. The world needs you and your contributions. You are bigger than your anxiety.

—Jon Patrick Hatcher

ABOUT THE AUTHORS

Thomas McDonagh is a licensed clinical psychologist who works in private practice in San Francisco. He started his training working with the general adult population, but quickly found he specifically enjoyed helping adults suffering with anxiety. A mutual friend introduced him to Jon, and after a period of collaboration, the foundation for this book and others was formed. Tom has received extensive training in evidence-based treatments, all of which make their way into the text.

Originally from the Midwest, Tom moved around the country for college and graduate work, including Vanderbilt University Medical Center in Nashville, Tennessee, and Kaiser Permanente Hospital in Santa Rosa, California. Readers will benefit from Tom's direct, problem-solving approach to anxiety issues.

A former curriculum developer and training manager by trade, **Jon Patrick Hatcher** left corporate life to pursue full-time nonfiction writing devoted to uniquely assisting those with life-altering adversities through irreverent humor and relatable content. As someone who personally rebounded from 13 sports-related surgeries, debilitating anxiety, and cancer, Jon is an expert at sourcing meaning in every challenge while helping others to leverage their own ability to overcome hardship. He holds an MA from Cal Poly, San Luis Obispo, and has spent years studying, utilizing, and sharing cognitive behavioral therapy (CBT), dialectical behavioral therapy (DBT), and exposure response prevention (ERP) techniques.

Jon doesn't dispense advice based on a single bad experience or being a self-proclaimed expert. Rather, his material is supported with abundant inquiry, empirical/clinical corroboration, and peer reviews. He currently resides in Campbell, California, with a Ficus tree and sister rescue cats, Thelma and Louise.